# WOMEN
## MAKE THE
# BEST
# SALESMEN

# WOMEN MAKE THE BEST SALESMEN

**Isn't It Time You Started Using Their Secrets?**

## Marion Luna Brem

CURRENCY
DOUBLEDAY

New York  London  Toronto  Sydney  Auckland

A CURRENCY BOOK
PUBLISHED BY DOUBLEDAY
a division of Random House, Inc.

CURRENCY is a trademark of Random House, Inc., and DOUBLEDAY
is a registered trademark of Random House, Inc.

WOMEN MAKE THE BEST SALESMEN was originally published in hardcover
by Currency in June 2004.

*Book design by Chris Welch*

Cataloging-in-Publication Data is on file with the Library of Congress
under the control number 2004-043857.

ISBN 0-385-51163-9

PRINTED IN THE UNITED STATES OF AMERICA

First Edition: June 2004
First Currency Paperback Edition: June 2005

All trademarks are the property of their respective companies

SPECIAL SALES
Currency Books are available at special discounts for bulk purchases for sales
promotions or premiums. Special editions, including personalized covers,
excerpts of existing books, and corporate imprints, can be created in large
quantities for special needs. For more information, write to Special Markets,
Currency Books, specialmarkets@randomhouse.com

3   5   7   9   10   8   6   4   2

*This book is dedicated*
*to*
*Isabella Antoinette Brem,*
*who was in development*
*at the same time as this book.*

# CONTENTS

PREFACE  WE'RE ALWAYS SELLING    xi

1 HOW SELLING SAVED MY LIFE  (and Can Energize Yours)    1

2 SALES 101: WHO AND WHAT ARE YOU REALLY SELLING?
(Hint: It's a Four-Letter Word)    9

3 DON'T COUNT ON PRODUCT KNOWLEDGE ALONE
TO MAKE THE SALE    13

4 DRESS THE PART (The "Three C's" of Making the Sale)    29

5 SET THE STAGE    39

6 MAKING A GOOD FIRST IMPRESSION LAST    51

7 IT'S ABOUT TIME    57

8 REFLECTED GLORY: USING OTHER PEOPLE'S ASSETS
TO STRENGTHEN YOURS    69

9 SELLING OUTSIDE YOUR "TERRITORY"    85

10 HOW TO COUNTER "I'M JUST LOOKING"    99

**11** YOU DON'T HAVE TO LIKE THEM—BUT *THEY* HAVE TO LIKE *YOU*   109

**12** TAKING CHARGE OF THE SALES PROCESS   123

**13** DETERMINING WHAT KIND OF BUYER YOU ARE SELLING TO   135

**14** WHAT YOU NEED TO KNOW ABOUT NEGOTIATING   147

**15** DEALING WITH DIFFICULT PEOPLE   159

**16** REJECTION: HOW TO LEARN FROM IT AND EARN FROM IT   175

**17** 12 SURE WAYS TO AVOID BLOWING A SALE   183

**18** 12 SURE WAYS TO IMPROVE YOUR SALES   193

**19** WHY WOMEN MAKE THE BEST SALESMEN   211

INDEX   217

# ACKNOWLEDGMENTS

Thank you, Tim Fitzmorris. I am so blessed to have you for my husband. I cherish the memory of sharing the silence and the space of our home office as I wrote this book.

Thank you, Brannon and Travis. It takes great courage for a son to choose to walk in the footsteps of his *mother*. You have both done so in a way that honors your own uniqueness.

Thank you, Sarah Brem, for being not only a wonderful daughter (in-law), but for also being a best friend. Your nurturing keeps me going.

Thank you, Mom, for believing I *should* have been first place even when I wasn't.

Thank you, Pa, for all the late nights at the kitchen table discussing everything from politics and religion to the importance of self-reliance and self-love.

And thank you, Mike Luna, for being the best brother a sister could wish for, not to mention soul mate.

Thank you, Dad, for showing me—by example—what a limitless profession selling can be.

Thank you, Gracie Perez and Mark Alaniz, and the rest of the "Love Gang" at Love Chrysler in Corpus Christi, Texas, and Love Chrysler Dodge Jeep in Alice, Texas. You are the best!

Thank you, Darold Adami, Jim Lindsey, and Dr. Noaman. When you couldn't help me solve a problem, you supported me. You embody true friendship.

Thank you, John Boswell. Your progressive thinking continues to amaze me. Thank you for so much—like introducing me to Roger Scholl at Random House. And thank you, Roger Scholl, for sharing my passion to get this book written. Thank you for sharing your resources. Thanks to all of you at Random House for all of the wonderful brainstorming, and the TLC you've given to my book. And Paul Brown, thank you for sharing your talent, wisdom, experience, and caring nature with me.

And finally, thank you to the many customers over the years who have allowed me to help them meet their transportation needs. I love you all!

# WE'RE ALWAYS SELLING

If you're alive, you're selling.

Whether you're obtaining a dinner reservation at a popular restaurant, seeking admission for your child to attend an exclusive private school, returning merchandise at a department store, dealing with a difficult person, bucking for a promotion at work, or literally involved with the selling of a product or service for a living, navigating your way through life requires an ability to promote yourself and persuade others of your point of view. And that's what sales is all about.

Because sales skills can be applied to so many facets of life, the more you develop them, the more you'll be able to get what you want out of life. Since none of us live our lives in total isolation—and who would want to even if we could?—we all have a vested interest in trying to get better at selling.

But sometimes it takes a while to understand that.

The first time I tried out my "if you're living, you're selling" concept, I was met with complete skepticism.

At an industrial trade show promoting our line of trucks, I ran into one of my former salesmen. He told me he had become a purchasing agent for a large corporation. As he put it, he was "so glad to be out of sales."

But he was still in sales, I told him. Sales included any exchange involving a relationship.

"I'm a buyer, not a seller," he said, adding that was part of the appeal of his new job. While he had learned a lot as one of our salesmen, he told me he thought he wasn't effective at it, and that is why he decided to change jobs.

The conversation moved on to some of the challenges he faced as a purchasing agent charged with saving his company money. "It's tough to please everyone. Employees want the best-quality products and managers want the best prices. And it's tough to persuade vendors to budge on either," he explained. As he talked more about what he did, however, he gradually realized that I was right.

Because his job involved relationships—which are *always* based on trades of some sort—he was, indeed, still a salesman.

"Don't tell anybody," he said, laughing.

Granted, the sales profession has suffered from a negative image. A single girlfriend once told me that she shied away from dating salesmen because she was afraid they'd be "too manipulative."

But today—especially with more women entering the sales profession—people are coming to realize that it is not about manipulation. Sales is about helping others. It is about persuasion through reason.

True selling is *not* the art of shading the truth to serve your own interests. It is about solving a customer's problem. If they benefit from the transaction, you will, too.

Selling always assumes give-and-take, which, if successful, results in making both lives better than they were before.

It is an art that transcends the world of revenues and commissions. It comes into play anytime there's a relationship.

Take marriage. One typical complaint wives have about their husbands is that they don't express their love often enough. "I told you I loved you on our wedding day. So what if that was forty years ago?" an old-timer repeatedly told his wife. "If anything changes, I'll tell you."

Here's a relationship that clearly illustrates that it's not good enough to just sit back on your laurels. In this example, the husband was trying to persuade his wife that she should only need to be sold *once* on his love for her. The husband probably truly believed that he had been a good husband by virtue of the fact that he had stuck around. From his perspective, he shouldn't have to promote or reaffirm his love for her.

"Why should I have to sell myself at all?" so many of us think to ourselves. "Shouldn't my work (a great personality, a sparkling intelligence, a steadfast loyalty) speak for itself?" Too often people feel hurt if they have to explicitly express what they feel should be obvious and understood. The truth, however, is that people need to be reminded of and shown occasionally that you value the relationship. Shining a light on yourself by pointing out what you feel and what you've done (and what you're capable of doing) is important. ("Getting noticed" is laid out as one of my basic principles in a later chapter.)

You don't have to raise your hand and say, "Hey, look at me."

No one likes a self-centered showoff. But saying, "Here's what I can do for you" can "shout" just as loudly.

One of the most common mistakes people make in selling is to try to act as if there's nothing in it for themselves. You don't have to hide the fact that you, too, benefit from a sale. Being forthright about that in your attitude and approach can help to establish a level of candor and trust with the other person. They expect that by selling something—including your own merits—you're going to benefit from doing so also. There is nothing wrong with acknowledging that.

Remember, each of us is *always* selling in one way or another. Everyone you interact with, everyone whose opinions and actions you affect, is a *customer* in your life. Skilled selling—the art of persuasion—is the one sure way to get more of what you want out of your life.

# Chapter 1

# HOW SELLING SAVED MY LIFE

(and Can Energize Yours)

Car salesmen. I admit it—they're often thought of as skirt-chasing, joke-telling, back-slapping, cigar-smoking deal makers. Why, then, at the age of thirty-two, did I, a wife, mother of two young sons, and a suburban homemaker, decide to join their ranks?

I had no choice.

I had just completed a six-month dose of commode-hugging chemotherapy. That horrible ordeal had followed back-to-back surgeries for two different cancers, cervical and breast.

Having a hysterectomy and a mastectomy within weeks of each other, and then having all my hair fall out as a result of chemo, had a devastating impact on my feminine psyche. I felt like less than a whole woman—and an extremely poor one at that. I had no health insurance and no savings.

Then things got worse.

The grueling stress brought about the end of my marriage.

And my prognosis wasn't good. The doctors gave me two to five years to live.

In a very short time I had lost so much. Most important of all, my self-esteem. I had no job, no husband, no medical coverage, and few of the resources necessary to build a career.

Moreover, I had my two boys, Brannon, age twelve, and Travis, seven, to raise. They needed me. But how could I support and care for them when I had such little work experience?

"You've always been good with people. Why don't you try sales?" my best friend, Susan, told me; she had been by my side throughout the whole ordeal.

Seven years earlier, I had fantasized about the possibility. I had taken a job as a switchboard operator at a high-volume car dealership in Dallas. For a stay-at-home mom, the job provided just the supplemental income we needed to move into a nicer neighborhood. I worked from five to nine P.M., Monday through Friday. It was perfect. My husband looked after the boys while I worked, we had a second income, and I got a bit of a "breather" from just being a mom.

Operating a switchboard, elevated like a throne in the middle of an automotive showroom, playing secretary to twenty flirtatious men, had made me feel like a prom queen. But prom queens, in my experience, aren't airheads. Watching our sales force at work, it didn't take me too many nights to realize that there was probably a better way to sell cars. I just didn't plan on showing them. After all, I had my life mapped out. With my boys both in school, I went back to college—I had lined up a scholarship—to obtain the computer science engineering degree that had been interrupted by motherhood.

So, while I was never serious about selling cars, the idea

entertained me during my quiet hours at the switchboard. How would I go about it?

I had noticed, for example, that often women were ignored when a couple came into the showroom. Of course, the salesmen would argue in their own defense that many of the women didn't have car-buying credit. But what the salesmen didn't seem to understand was that these same women had veto power. If they didn't like the car, the deal, or even the salesman, there would be no sale, regardless of the enthusiasm of their husband or boyfriend. If I were in the salesman's place, I would divide my attention equally between the couple. Moreover, I saw car salesmen pressuring customers into making a deal regardless of whether or not the car fit their needs or budget. They were focused solely on their monthly sales quota rather than on building a lifetime customer relationship.

I had put my early observations of sales on a shelf in the back of my mind while I concentrated on my marriage and raising our sons. But I found those observations resurfacing once again as I searched within myself for a way to rebound from cancer, divorce, and financial devastation.

"Car sales. Okay—I'll give it a shot," I told Susan.

## 1.1 Getting Hired—the Ultimate Sale

I started my job hunt by cold calling. "If one door doesn't open," I told myself, "knock on another." So I did. The first sixteen remained shut.

On my seventeenth try, a door opened. But only a little.

The sales manager I was interviewing with said to me, "I've been thinking about hiring a broad. And you seem like the nervy type," he went on. "Okay—let's see how it works out."

I had asked for a sales job with no sales experience. I suppose on the surface it *did* take nerve. But I had believed in what I was selling—myself. I knew that my homemaker's résumé—though it wouldn't look impressive on paper—was strong. For me, I didn't feel that I should be hired *in spite of* having homemaking experience, but rather that I should be hired *because of* my homemaking experience. For starters, I was experienced in problem solving, time management, budgeting, priority setting, space planning, and negotiation. For years, I had been creating and seizing opportunities to make life better for my family. In fact, I had centered my life around taking care of others. I recalled how I was able to persuade the principal at my younger son's elementary school to transfer him from morning to afternoon kindergarten (after initially being turned down). How I successfully coached my ex-husband to seek a promotion at work. How I was able to obtain medical treatment on nothing more than my promise to pay.

I did have sales experience, and that is what I communicated to my first "customer" in my new career—the man who decided (reluctantly) to hire me.

As much as I believed in myself, my first year in car sales taught me more. I learned, for example, that I could get up after a fall. Literally. One time, rushing out to greet a customer, I tripped and landed facedown in the middle of a flower bed.

Moments before, having just received another sales rejection via telephone, I gazed at the huddle of eight or nine salesmen standing outside the showroom. Should I make an effort to join them? From my peripheral vision, I spotted a middle-aged couple walking toward the new cars. Somehow the couple had escaped the attention of the salesmen. Walking briskly toward them, I cut through a flower bed to save time. I tripped on a loose stone and found myself with my skirt up, one knee bleeding through my pantyhose, and one of my high heels broken off my muddied shoe.

Before I could get up, another salesman had introduced himself to the couple.

Though I felt as crushed as the flowers I was lying on, I got up and dusted myself off. I had to—I had two sons to support. But it was a lesson in resiliency. After repairing my shoe, my skinned knee, and my bruised feelings, I went on to sell three cars that day.

By the end of the year, I had applied some of the ideas I had developed about sales and had learned some new ones. And I had earned the "Salesman of the Year" honor along with a trip to the Super Bowl and a men's Rolex watch. (It never occurred to management that a woman would win.)

Within five years of selling my first car, I had founded my first auto dealership, Love Chrysler Inc., in Corpus Christi, Texas. Refining my sales and customer skills further, I soon opened a second dealership and developed ownership stakes in several other businesses.

Since then, I have been honored with awards and accolades beyond my wildest dreams. My story has been profiled in countless newspapers and magazines and on national radio and television talk shows. And now I want to share with you what I've used to make it all happen.

For those of you who are women, perhaps like me your homemaking résumé is your starting point. Others may be farther along. There are tips here that will prove useful to you men, as well. Some of you may not be interested in a career in sales at all—but I guarantee that you, too, will find this book valuable. After all, we're all selling ourselves throughout our lives, whether we're trying to get our child into a special program, find a lifetime partner, look for a job, or return merchandise to a store. Whatever your goal, you'll be able to seize new opportunities to improve your life by applying the sales skills I discuss in the following pages. Because we're all "salesmen" at heart. And once you know how to sell *yourself*, you can do anything!

## 1.2   Not Knowing How to Sell Is Risky

Like a drowning woman, I reached out to sales as a life preserver, and it saved my life. But you don't have to be drowning to experience the thrill of being a top salesperson. Few professions offer more income potential, job security, and work benefits. No other skill offers more potential for self-improvement and relationship enhancement.

Think about it. In a downturned economy, who has more job security? The salesperson who's generating an income for the company, or the person who's considered an expense?

If you put in the effort, selling is not risky; it is secure living. It offers the only pay plans that don't have a cap. All it takes is a bit of faith—belief in yourself and your product.

If I seem like somewhat of a missionary for sales, I suppose I am. I once heard a car salesman say, "I peddle metal." Well, I disagree. To the extent I do "peddle" anything, I sell helpfulness and solutions. That to me is the heart of the sales experience. That's what a good salesperson really does—identifies a need and fills it. I've based my professional career on the belief that making people happy and making money are compatible with each other. My motto is "Help others to help yourself." I believe that's the mission of the true sales hero.

I'm excited about sharing what I've learned from my life in sales. Whether you're reading this book to improve your career in sales or to become more of a driver in your life, the principles are the same. Selling cars was the vehicle (no pun intended) I happened to use to learn the art of persuasion. I had no idea in those early days just how far my atlas of information would take me. Sales saved my life, and it can energize yours, too!

> ■ **Everybody has sales experience they can draw on.** Think of five times in your life you were able to change someone's mind or have them adopt your point of view. What did those successes all have in common? How can you use the same approach in and outside of your job?
>
> ■ **Think of the best salespeople you have encountered as a customer.** What made them good? What can you borrow from them to improve your life?
>
> ■ **Selling, even if you don't do it for a living, opens up limitless possibilities.** We're all "salesmen" in one way or another. I truly believe that if you know how to sell, you can do anything.

# Chapter 2

# SALES 101: WHO AND WHAT ARE YOU REALLY SELLING?

## (Hint: It's a Four-Letter Word)

A customer, in the traditional sense, is someone who buys a product or a service. We've all been customers. But because I've taken the buy/sell concept one step further by showing that we're all in sales, I feel compelled to expand the definition of "customer" as well.

A customer is anyone who is on the receiving end of a persuasion. To prove the point, let me give you an extreme example. If I have just persuaded you to allow me to cut in front of your car before you proceed at a stoplight, you are a customer. You have acquiesced to my request. You have "bought" into it.

Anyone you have a relationship with whose actions and/or opinions affect you is a customer in your life. And the relationship need not be a lifelong one; it may be only a passing one.

By this redefinition, prospective customers are all around us. I'm not suggesting that you travel through life figuring out how you can use people to your best advantage. But I am saying that sales opportunities, broadly defined, are present throughout our everyday lives.

Let's say you want your husband to join you in taking dance lessons. Or you desire an audition for the lead role in an upcoming stage play. Or you want a store manager to discount a slightly damaged leather coat. When you possess and properly use polished sales skills, the possibilities for improving your world are infinite.

Because *my* world is one where buying and selling products and services is my everyday business, the following material will often be presented in terms of traditional sales. Therefore, I invite you to open up your imagination to draw your own corollaries between the techniques I offer and your own life circumstances.

## 2.1 What You Are Really Selling

"Help me."

That's what a good salesperson hears every time a customer approaches. Whether you are selling cars, cosmetics, engineering services, Tupperware, or tubular steel—or your own services such as when you apply for a job—what you're really selling is H-E-L-P. You are either solving a problem or satisfying a need.

As dramatic as it may sound, every salesperson helps their customers improve their life. And that's true whether you are a national sales manager for a Fortune 100 company or a waitress at the local diner.

Take the example of a motorist asking to cut in front of you. Let's assume I'm the motorist seeking to cut into the line of traffic. For you to allow it, I have to communicate to you somehow that by helping me, you'll benefit too. In this case, I am limited to using only facial expressions, and perhaps a bit of finger-pointing and lip-synching, to make my case. First comes the request—the "please" part. Next, assuming I get the go-ahead, a quick nod or wave to indicate "thank you." If you acquiesce to my request for your help, you can expect to experience at least two good feelings as well—the sense of pride that follows having done a good deed and a sense of being appreciated. And with that, you are likely to have a better day, too!

## 2.2   How Will This Benefit Me?

The point is: Whatever's being given to a customer has always got to be worth more in their mind than what they have "paid," whether in cash, time, or something else. When you offer something that helps your customer to look or feel good, you've taken the first step toward sales success.

The first time I failed to recognize this important principle, I hit a brick wall.

I had been selling cars at the same dealership for about two years, when a management position in the finance department opened up. By then the physical demand of selling cars—the leg and back pain that came from pounding the pavement every day, along with the discomfort of working in record-setting temperatures—had taken its toll on me. So I decided to ask for the management job. But that was only part of the reason I decided to pursue a job in management. I had consistently "led the board" (sold more cars than any of my twenty colleagues), and I felt I had earned this promotion.

And so I told my boss that I wanted the promotion, that I deserved it.

Imagine my surprise when I heard him reply, "I'd be a fool to promote you. You're my top gun in sales." He went on to tell me how important I was to him on the "floor"—the showroom floor sales area. Paralyzed by his reaction, I was struck dumb. I had temporarily lost my ability to persuade, to sell. The fact that a finance manager is responsible for selling extended warranties in a car dealership, among other products, never even occurred to me. The fact that my car-selling experience was the perfect preparation for selling products in the new position never occurred to me. The fact that I could add a great deal as a finance manager to his bottom line never occurred to me. All I could think about was that he had let me down. I felt hurt. I felt rejected. It wasn't until much later—after leaving—that I realized I had failed to point out how *I* could help *him*.

Ironically, that botched sale—when I should have been selling my boss on how I could help his business do better—came at a time when I was enjoying a great many successes in my career. Although I was a top sales pro, I had overlooked the most basic premise in selling: Always show your customer how your product can help them.

I've never forgotten it since.

---

- **Think of a customer as anyone who is in a position to affect your life.**
- **Selling is the art of helping** . . . of solving other people's problems. "Help," "solve," "needs" are the key words that represent the essence of selling.
- **"How will this benefit me?"** is the big question in a customer's mind, even if they never ask it out loud. Deliver the answer up front.

---

# Chapter 3

# DON'T COUNT ON PRODUCT KNOWLEDGE ALONE TO MAKE THE SALE

To know how your product can fit into a customer's life-style, satisfy his or her needs, and fulfill his or her hopes and dreams, you must first know your product. Cold.

In sales, your product is your partner. Being intimately familiar with it is essential to helping your customer. You can't meet your customer's needs if you don't fully understand what you have to offer them.

One of the most likable car salesmen I ever worked with never understood this simple concept. Abundantly talented, he had, as his peers put it, "the gift of gab." Personally, I loved being around him. He had a collection of one-liners that would rival any stand-up comedian's. He was the type of guy who never knew a stranger and seemed comfortable in any setting.

Yet, with all of his natural abilities, he never excelled in sales. One day, it became clear what was missing. "These cars are all pretty much alike," I overheard him tell a customer. "They all even have the same great smell inside of them."

He was virtually cruising right past the part where customers become familiar with the product and how it can improve their life. Customers were entertained by him. Customers liked him. But because he never explained any of the functions of the equipment on the cars, they never got to know how owning one could make their lives better. So they never bought from him.

To help your customer, you first need to know your product inside and out. Period.

## 3.1    You Must Know More Than the Specs

Products and services are rarely just about themselves. There are also warranties, financing terms, delivery schedules, and the like. If you are applying for a job, there are all the ancillary concerns beyond just doing the job well—how well you get along with the others on staff, whether you are likely to stay in the position for a reasonable length of time, or whether you are likely to become restless and expect rapid advancement. To be successful in sales, you need to master them all. After all, how can a client rely on you to help them weigh their options if you don't know what the options are or how they work?

To expect to close a sale, you may also need to explain *how* a product can be acquired.

Just the other day, a saleslady at a cosmetic counter disappeared without a word after she took my purchase-to-be out of the display case. She was gone for a long time. At one point, I wondered if some emergency had called her away. Then, out of the blue, she appeared with my purchase in a bag and the total price. It was only *after* I commented on her disappearance that she explained that she had gone to a nearby cash register (located out of my view). What she hadn't realized was that she had almost lost me as a customer because she neglected to explain the simple process of consummating the transaction.

Whether you've just shown a home to your prospective client, or broached the subject of marriage to your boyfriend, mapping out the way to get there is helpful for both to gain the other person's understanding and advance your cause.

An old friend of mine complained to me that her live-in boyfriend was never going to propose to her, so she finally proposed to him. She laid out a simple plan for a combination wedding/honeymoon getaway—just the two of them. And he loved it! Later he admitted that it wasn't the idea of marriage that had scared him, but rather the thought of a big, "complicated" wedding (which she never wanted anyway). The more misconceptions and unknowns you can remove from your prospect's thinking, the more likely they'll be to move forward.

It's important to remember that you sell your product more often than your customer purchases it. What may be an everyday business event to you (*selling* homes, software, consulting services, tax advice, loans, or whatever) is probably, on the flip side (*buying* homes, software, consulting services, tax advice, loans, or whatever), a special and even unique experience for your customer. I used to sell seven to ten cars per week. But I always reminded myself that my customers probably didn't buy that many in a lifetime. Because of that, each time I walked the buyer *slowly* through every step in the process, from the moment he said, "I'll take it," to the point where I handed him the keys. I made sure he understood not only all the features of the car but how it might be financed, how long it would take for us to get it ready for him, what was involved in getting it registered, and so on. The key here: Never assume your customer understands the process of becoming an owner.

I consistently stress to our salespersons that they shouldn't stop short at just memorizing and explaining the specs of the cars. If they don't explain to a customer *how* they can end up driving one home, their product knowledge falls short of being helpful.

I'll never forget the time early in my career when I made a follow-up call to a prospective customer, only to learn that she had purchased a car from my competitor. The woman told me that she had chosen them over me because they could provide her with "one-stop shopping." She went on to tell me that they were a "contracting agent" for the credit union. That meant, she explained, that she could execute all of the documents pertaining to the financing of the car at the dealership, which would save her a trip to the credit union. I could have kicked myself— of course, I could have offered her that same convenience! I was a contracting agent, too. All new-car dealerships are. But because I didn't tell her that, I lost the sale. If you don't communicate what you know and show how you can help the customer, all the product knowledge in the world isn't going to help you. Successful selling is much more than just understanding the function of all of the knobs and buttons.

There are also the nuances of knowing when and how your knowledge should be used. My experience has taught me to use it selectively, most often in response to a customer's specific concerns or questions. Otherwise, you can come off sounding like a know-it-all—and one who is out of touch with your customer's needs at that. You don't need to demonstrate how smart and how knowledgeable you are. Customers will be able to tell that for themselves by the thorough way you answer whatever questions they ask of you.

In the first month of my sales career, as a woman in a male-dominated field, I felt likely to be continually challenged on product knowledge. So I armed myself, memorizing fuel capacity, the exact size of the trunk space, horsepower, wheelbase of each model, and so on. You name it, I knew it. Eager to display my training, I popped the hood on a new car in the course of a product demonstration to a sweet senior-aged couple. My presentation was peppered with facts. No sooner had I begun reciting the fuel-injection data than the woman looked at her husband and said, "I'll wait inside."

I had lost her. (And I knew she was a key part of the buying decision; that meant I had lost the sale as well.) I may as well have been speaking Japanese as far as trying to connect with her needs and concerns.

What I hadn't done in presenting the product's features was to translate what those features could mean to the couple. For example, the exceptional fuel capacity of the car meant they could make a round-trip visit to their grandchildren without having to stop for gas. But instead of pointing that out, and trying to connect what I was selling to my customers' lives, I had simply said, "This gas tank holds twenty-two point seven gallons." So what? My clumsy and inappropriate use of product knowledge cost me a sale.

But it did teach me a valuable lesson. From then on, *I always made a point of translating the specs into terms meaningful to my customer.*

This mistake, by the way, is a common one in all sorts of jobs and situations. How much more helpful it is when that information is translated for us. My financial planner recently did exactly that when explaining an insurance policy she thought I needed.

"This new term policy," she told me, "guarantees you no increases in premium during expansion plans for your business." As I heard her explanation, I felt peace of mind settle over me. She had explained her insurance product to me in a way that I was able to grasp and appreciate immediately.

> ## 3.2   Know Your Inventory:
> ## Put Yourself in Your Customer's Shoes

As a consumer, when I'm about to buy something, when I have already made the commitment to open my purse, I feel so disappointed when I hear apologies such as "Sorry, I didn't realize we're out of that color," or "I could have sworn we had that model in," or "My computer must be wrong." Those words are about as welcome as a "wrong number" during dinner.

And if you think an offer of "We can order it" is helpful, think about the instant-gratification world we live in. The only time we can even afford to overnight something anymore is when we have plenty of time.

When a customer has taken mental ownership of a product, they have embarked on an emotional experience. That's why it is such a wrenching time for you, as a salesperson, to deliver one of those apologetic "I'm so sorry" comments. You need to understand that you have caused your customer to feel emotional pain, the pain of having lost something. Rather than walking out of the store with the cherished and needed item, they walk away frustrated, grasping for a way to come to terms with the fact that they weren't able to get what they wanted. And you can be sure *you* have also lost something—the trust of your customer. It's tough to regain it. Even if you try to be helpful by offering a "plan B," your customer is now distrustful.

Knowing what you have available *before* you raise the hopes and dreams of your customer can prevent these happenings. Having that knowledge makes you aware of not only what *is* available but also what *isn't*.

There's nothing more frustrating than finding a requested item after the customer has left.

The decision on the part of the customer to buy something means taking a leap of faith. Asking your customer to take a second leap of faith—after you've delivered anything short of their expectation—is like getting them to leap off a cliff. In their new mind-set, it's too risky. The enticement can almost never be big enough. Why? Because it's too late.

Customers who can count on their salesperson to know what they have and sell them what they need are repeat customers. They come back again and again because of the strength of the relationship you have forged. When customers can't depend on you, you look unprofessional in their eyes. And who wants to buy from someone like that? Work hard at being someone customers can depend on. One simple way to do that is to stay on top of your inventory and services.

## WALK THE LOT

When I was a salesperson selling cars (before I bought my first dealership), I made a regular habit of "walking the lot." In addition to running into unattended customers, my walk taught me a great deal. I saw which models we had plenty of and which ones were scarcer. I had first look at the trade-ins. And I got to learn firsthand about new models hot off the truck. I say "firsthand" because that's exactly what it was. Mine was usually the first hand placed on the hood of each new car. I became known as the dealership's data bank of inventory information, because I knew more about all the cars on the lot than anyone else there.

My fellow salesmen (who were also my competitors, since we were all in pursuit of the "Top Salesman of the Month" plaque and the perks that came with it) would often come up to me and ask, "Marion, do we still have that red Cherokee?" Their customers would look at them with an annoyed "Why don't you know?" glare. They'd start to wonder whether they wouldn't have been better off coming to me in the first place. And when recommending a salesperson to their friends, you can be sure it was my name more often than not that was passed around.

The practice of "walking the lot" is virtually the same no matter what business you're in. Do you sell houses? Then find out which hot properties have offers pending, as well as the status and quality of those offers. In that way, your client can make more informed decisions. They may elect to propose a "backup offer" on a pending property or move on to something else altogether.

Perhaps you're selling an intangible like homeowner's insurance. Are you sure the coverage you've been touting is available for the particular locale of the homeowner? Hurricane protection? What are the details, the fine print? Can they get flood insurance on this property? Walk *your* lot.

Again, this is a good practice no matter what you sell. I was sold on a hot new coral lip shade the other day at a department store after receiving a mini-makeover. "I have the lipstick, but it seems I don't have the pencil liner," the apologetic makeup artist told me. Why had she teased me like that? I was so annoyed that I walked out without buying anything. If she had "walked the lot," so to speak, before she offered to make me up, I wouldn't have been disappointed.

Years ago, I called a sales meeting to fire up my sales force. "We've got a strong advertising campaign coming up," I told them. "We've even got a spot during one of the local breaks on the Super Bowl."

Shortly after the meeting, I got a call from the account executive at the station. "It turns out I can't get you on the Super Bowl," she told me. "Seems we sold out last week."

Wow, I was so upset. She had caused me to look flaky in the eyes of my sales staff. It was a long time before I could trust anything she said.

The point is, do your homework. Don't excite clients with a product only to play takeaway later. They will feel robbed if you do.

---

## 3.3   Be a Mind Reader

Let me make something clear. It's not just 80 percent of the car-buying decisions that are made by women. It's 80 percent of *all* buying decisions that are made or greatly influenced by women. If you're not selling to women, you're probably not successful.

So if women are doing most of the buying, and women love to be surprised (I know I do, and so do most of the women I know), a good salesperson should set out to be a mind reader, and provide them with exactly the right product, one that will make them feel good about themselves.

Relax—it's easier than you think. Men think we're complicated. They've written books about how to deal with us, as if we're from another planet (Venus, if I remember correctly). They would prefer it if we came equipped with owner's manuals. But when it comes to gifts, most women's response is "If I have to spell out for you exactly what I want, it's not the same." And it's not.

That's probably why we "hint." It feels better when someone delivers something to us that we didn't have to come right out and ask for. It shows the other person is thinking about us.

Most women know this intuitively, and all women who work as salespeople should take advantage of it when it comes to selling. A local boutique capitalizes on this hint-giving notion by actually going so far as to provide a forum for women on how to give their husbands or partners hints. The store hosts an annual "couples" cocktail reception—complete with hors d'oeuvres—three weeks before Christmas. It's a perfect setting for their female customers to "drop hints" to their husbands or boyfriends about what would make a great Christmas present.

At last year's event, I heard one man say to the person greeting new arrivals at the reception, "I brought my checkbook like a good husband." In other words, it's not exactly a secret what is going on. (My husband claims he saw one wife give hand signals to her saleslady.)

Nevertheless, the event's success stems from the twin realities that (a) women need help in guiding their husbands toward pleasing them, and (b) the husbands seem to welcome the help. (I should add that under my own Christmas tree last year was a gorgeous suede jacket that I just happened to try on that night.)

When dealing with customers, however, such hints aren't always revealed so obviously. That's why it's not enough to listen to what the customer says he or she wants. You have to listen *for* hints—even the ones customers aren't aware of themselves.

The saleswoman who sold us a swimming pool understood this perfectly. In the process of comparing one pool company proposal with another, we asked this woman to get back to us after she had specced out and priced what we told her we wanted.

She came back with the response to what we told her we wanted. But, after presenting us with that, she whipped out an elaborate lifelike drawing of a modified pool, showing a bar setup and round tables placed throughout the yard. Every detail in her presentation tickled my love for entertaining, a love she must have picked up on when we talked about the kind of pool we wanted. And her second proposal was priced comparably to the first, because she made concessions in areas less important to us (like the depth of the pool).

Was I surprised.

I hadn't realized what had been bothering me about the pool project until she addressed it—that it needed to serve as a kind of entertainment center. How did she know? When I asked her, she explained that I had mentioned how, fearing we could not accommodate large parties with a pool, we had put the project on hold until after we had hosted my son's wedding reception. Acting on her intuition—I think of it as drawing on her excellent sales skills—she came up with a design for more than just a pool. She created an entertainment and activity center where the pool was the showpiece.

Her plan would not only have accommodated the wedding reception, it would have turned it into a celebrity affair!

Wowing your customer sometimes requires that you "take the liberty" of delivering more than they expect. To do that, you've got to be able to anticipate their wants and needs. Don't wait for them to give you paint-by-number instructions. Chances are they won't, and even if they do, they may welcome suggestions that go beyond what they've outlined.

If you are a woman, you have an innate advantage when it comes to this. After all, if you're good at *giving* hints, you're probably pretty good at picking up on them.

The pool saleslady picked up on the fact that I felt I was going to have to compromise on the way I like to entertain by adding a pool to our backyard, although I never came out and said so. She did this by really listening to what I was saying, as well as what I didn't say.

I think of this as "listening hard." Listening to not only what's said but also what's *not* said. The pool saleslady did what any of us can do. Sensing that I was less excited about the project than I should be, she set out to learn why. By actively listening, she got me talking. She soon picked up clues leading to a revelation—for both of us.

Such hints come in many forms. Some businesses have been successful at setting up what I call no-brainer systems for interpreting and storing hints, enabling them to offer a bit more assistance than just order taking. I was impressed by one such business the other night when I called in an order for pizza.

If you're like me, pizza ordering is usually more spontaneous than planned. (Who says, "Next Wednesday, the thirteenth, we're going to order pizza for dinner"?) And so, responding to an unexpected night of entertaining, I dialed the number before I had determined exactly what I was going to order. The young lady on the other end of the line made it easy. "For starters, may I suggest our hot wings? You ordered them last month."

"That's a great idea," I responded. It was simple. The orders I had placed in the past were recorded to help me place my future ones.

In my business, I've been able to apply the mind-reader concept in many ways, but they all have one thing in common: Like the pizza place, when Love Chrysler does the asking, it's not "What would you like us to offer?" but rather "Would you like some of what we have to offer?"

For example, our "We love your kids" play center was created in anticipation of the question "Would you like some help with your kids so that you can concentrate on shopping for a car?" (Heaven forbid a mother visiting one of my dealerships should have to ask her salesperson for a piece of paper that her three-year-old could draw on.) After all, what we're really selling is H-E-L-P, and there's nothing worse for a mom shopping for anything she needs (or someone trying to sell to that mom) than an unhappy three-year-old.

But we go one step beyond merely helping. We constantly update the toys in the toy center so that the kids won't be bored when they come back. (We have a lot of repeat customers, and we would like to keep it that way.)

We also make note of what radio station a customer's trade-in is tuned to. That way when they get into their new car for the first time, the radio has been set to the same station. It's these kind of small "mind-reading" gestures that communicate to a customer that you care about them.

Another application of our "mind reading" came about as a result of an article I read in a trade magazine that stated that women typically pay more for cars than men do. (No wonder a national survey revealed that women said they'd rather get a root canal than go car shopping.) In response to this inequity, once a year we close our dealership for business and host a "How to Buy a Car" clinic for ladies only.

The showroom is cleared to accommodate as much seating as possible, the salespersons are given the night off, and the outside experts are brought in. Typically, we'll invite a loan officer from a local bank who offers tips on credit and explains how loan terms work, a representative from the Better Business Bureau serving up information on consumer rights (Lemon Law, etc.), and other professionals. I act as hostess and MC, but nothing more. In addition to the information we provide, we offer dinner buffet-style (food that can be eaten on a lap during the presentation) and, of course, child care.

The only challenge has been space. Last time we held a clinic, we had so many attendees that I got a friendly hint from the fire marshal that the next time I held the clinic I might want to rent out a hall (or limit attendance).

This is but one of the ways I try to transform the mind-set at my dealerships from one of being in the car business to one of being in the pleasing business.

These ideas come from a place we can all tap into: intuition and imagination. You always want to ask, "What would I like if I were sitting on the other side of the desk?" "What would 'Wow!' me?" Don't wait until your customers ask you.

That's why I don't recommend focus groups. They're about as romantic as a woman giving her husband or boyfriend a

"Here's what I want" list. After all, if customers have to come right out and tell me everything they want, how can they experience their purchase as something more than expected?

I know we've got to do more than satisfy our customers. We've got to "Wow!" them. To do that, I've got to be a mind reader. And you can be, too.

---

■ **Know your product.** It's the most basic preparation you can make to be an effective salesperson and best help your customer. Present your product in ways that have real meaning to your customers' lives.

■ **Know your inventory.** Don't risk disappointing your customer and losing credibility by presenting a product they can't walk out the door with.

■ **Be a mind reader.** Look for hints—spoken and unspoken—to offer your customers more than they expect.

# Chapter 4

# DRESS THE PART
## (The "Three C's" of Making the Sale)

D ress appropriately."
"Dress for success."
There's a whole industry out there that tells how those striving to get ahead should dress. The advice for women ranges from "Make sure your hair is clean and coiffed" (what on earth is "coiffed," anyway?) to "Make sure your hemline reaches the floor when you're kneeling" (what kind of sales position calls for a woman to be on her knees?).

But as tired as all this may be, I cannot write a book about sales without at least touching upon the subject of clothes.

## 4.1 Dress for Comfort (Yours and Theirs)

Dressing appropriately begins with dressing comfortably for your sake *and* your customer's. I'm a bit of a shoe junkie. Just the other day, I met my husband for lunch. As we were walking from the parking lot to the restaurant, he asked, "Are those shoes comfortable to walk in?" (They were four-inch heels.)

"No," I admitted. "But they're sexy. Don't you think?"

"Not really," he responded. He went on to tell me that his feet were hurting just *looking* at how uncomfortable I was. He was right. Dressing uncomfortably is like yawning. It's contagious. It can affect all those around you. And it's tough to sell anything to a customer who's feeling uncomfortable on your behalf. (And yes, in a sense, my husband *is* my customer, since I care about his opinion. So I need to make him feel comfortable as well.)

Comfort begins with proper sizing, certainly. But there's more to a good fit than just wearing the right size. For one, comfort also considers climate. Are you selling indoors or outdoors? Selling cars in scorching Texas heat, for example, made it easy for me to realize that the idea of a navy-blue suit commonly suggested by well-meaning advisers wasn't a good choice. On those days when I was selling outdoors and temperatures hit triple digits, I opted for lighter colors and a more casual feel. My customers were suffering from the heat, too, and the last thing they needed was to see me wilting.

Dressing appropriately for the weather is a plus in sales because it also projects an image of you as a sensible person. It reminds me of a misjudgment made by a female journalist I saw last winter on television. Conducting an interview outdoors on a bitterly cold morning, she was dressed professionally and fashionably but in nothing more than a chic suit. She looked painfully foolish as she stood shivering and wincing, determined to grin and bear the freezing winds. I was in agony just watching her, and finally changed the channel.

You, too, have an audience every time you're engaged in an interaction. The person across from you may not have a remote control with which to change the channel, but I can assure you, they will tune your message out if they witness you in discomfort. To influence someone, you first have to have their attention.

## 4.2 Dress Compatibly

Dressing compatibly with your clientele and your product is an important part of the bonding process for women in general, and it's certainly true in sales. A very young drug-company rep made this discovery as she was attempting to persuade her medical clients that she was a credible agent for her product. Though she knew the drugs' chemical components and capabilities forward and backward, she kept running into what she called "blow-off rejection." She thought her lack of success had to do with her gender and age; she was struggling to make sales. I suggested to her that she should replace her playful sundresses and strappy sandals with more basic, professional pieces. She had been dressing as if she were selling condos in Cancún rather than pharmaceuticals in Philadelphia. Her fun attire, even in hot summer months, wasn't compatible with her serious product or her mature clientele. In fact, it undercut the message about herself that she was trying to convey.

Simply put, she didn't fit the image of the medical profession. (Her gender and young age may have been two strikes against her, but she didn't need three.) She listened to what I had to say, and went on to become the youngest—and first woman—sales manager in the company.

People prefer to deal with someone they see as being "like" them (which may explain why a technology consultant, about to make his pitch to me in my office the other day, pointed to the photos of my two sons on my desk and told me he also had two boys).

Think about it. Men have sold legal services, insurance plans, and ideas on the golf courses for years. That's because golfers like doing business with other golfers. The more aligned you can be with your client's life, the more connected they're apt to feel to you. The way you dress is a subtle but effective way to show "I'm one of you."

I'm in no way suggesting that you should become a clone of anyone else. Stay within your personal comfort and taste range. Fortunately, I've discovered my range to be wide. (And I bet yours is, too.) Just as I'm multilingual and a multitasker, I'm a multidresser. In my early days as a CEO, I drew upon this resource quite effectively.

When I opened my first dealership, one of the actions I took was to conduct weekly, early-morning shop meetings with my (all male) technicians to get their input on improvements to the service department. At first, these reach-out meetings weren't effective. Nothing more than a few superficial, polite exchanges took place. Then I changed the time and place of the meetings. I started having them after work at a local hamburger joint. That improved the communication somewhat, but I still couldn't get them to open up completely.

After a couple of weeks, I began going home before the meeting to change from my business suit to blue jeans. I couldn't believe the difference! Was this the same group of guys? I had loosened my tie, so to speak, and they felt as if I was someone they could relate to. And all it took to wake their spirits *up* was for me to dress *down*. And I didn't compromise myself one bit.

## 4.3   Dress Confidently

For those of you who are women, if you were like me, when you were a young teenager you probably called a girlfriend or two at night to find out what she was going to be wearing the next day to school. That's because, as young teens, we craved a sense of belonging. We crave it as adults, as well. There's nothing wrong with wanting to fit in. In fact, when we do, we're actually inviting the people around us to feel comfortable, in part because we feel comfortable, but also because we're showing them that we agree with their choices.

But as flattering as imitation is, you never want to carry it so far that you lose who you are in the process. When we mimic someone else's style and abandon our own—and you'll know it if you do—we sell ourselves short. And our self-confidence is usually the casualty. Let me explain.

As very young children (say, ages three to nine), virtually all of us were extraordinarily creative. We'd dance around the room, sing songs, recite poems, do acrobatics, put on plays—anything to get attention. "Foolish" wasn't part of our vocabulary; nor was the word "conformity." Then, sometime during our teen years, Miss Show-off became Miss Copycat. (Think of all the teenage Britney Spears look-alikes and wannabes out there.) Suddenly we obsessed about what everyone thought of us. It was safer to become "one of" so we wouldn't stick out. We went beyond wanting to fit in. It was as if we didn't want to be noticed.

And so our creativity was stifled. Our individuality and sense of self was lost. And with no sense of self, there can be no *self-confidence*. (It's no wonder adolescent girls all too often struggle with self-esteem issues.)

In sales, it's important to be yourself. Accordingly, your own style should be reflected in your dress. I believe you can be compatible with your climate, your product, your customers, *and* yourself. Think of Katharine Hepburn, who embraced her own style by bringing slacks for women into vogue. In being a bold trendsetter, she caught the eye of many, but not their wrath.

Attention is a good thing. (Throughout these pages, you'll hear me advocating stand-out-from-the-pack ways of doing things.) I believe dressing in a manner that commands attention—in the form of admiration and respect—is a very good thing. But the way you dress should not offend your customer. (And as I've already noted, women are the primary customers in this country.)

Let's face it; we're all fashion critics of one another. A low-cut blouse or a skirt that's too short can be toxic to even the best sales presentation. Sexual seduction has its place and time—but the sales desk isn't the place, and *never* in sales is there a time. Competing with your outfit for attention crosses the line between attraction and distraction. And competing with a female customer for her man's attention crosses the line between relationship success and relationship suicide. Having good taste and "class" is about staying true to yourself while ensuring that you're not creating negative vibes for your customer or anyone else whose opinion you value.

I have to confess that there was one time when I tossed caution to the wind to follow my own best judgment.

I recall it vividly. My first sales manager had recently cautioned me about wearing red. He said it was a turnoff to customers because it made a woman appear to be too bold, hostile, and aggressive. Intuitively, I didn't agree. I love red, and I felt it could be worn in good taste.

But new to sales, I didn't want to offend my boss, and so for the longest time I didn't wear red.

One day (with a pretty good track record of selling in place), feeling a bit brave, I put on a bright, candy-apple-red suit that had been collecting dust in the back of my closet. It had been an old favorite of mine, but I had put it away after hearing the sales manager's comment. The day I wore it to work, I went on to have a fabulous sales day. Everything I touched turned to gold. It wasn't that I had an "I'll show him" attitude that fueled my day; rather, it was how red made me *feel*. Authentic. Energetic. Confident. I was moving like a woman who was on her way to the top of the world. Nor did I offend anyone along the way.

And that, I'm convinced, is the key to dressing for sales, or appropriately for any affair—dressing in a way that makes you feel good about yourself without alienating the very people you care about impressing.

When you feel that you look good, you feel good. And when you feel good, chances are you'll *do* good.

### SUMMING UP

I believe dressing is such a personal matter that no one should tell another what's absolutely right or wrong. And I certainly don't proclaim to be a fashion expert. But these principles—

dressing comfortably, compatibly, and confidently—are worth paying attention to, whatever you do for a living.

Put the "Three C's" to the test:

- **The comfort test:** All things being equal, whom would you more likely buy from—the lady selling insurance who's annoyed with and constantly adjusting her bra strap, or the one who's not distracted in any way and therefore is able to offer you her full attention?
- **The compatibility test:** All things being equal, whom would you more likely buy from—a woman selling high-end cosmetics who looks as if she just got out of bed, or the woman sporting a tasteful application of the latest shades of her product line?
- **The confidence test:** All things being equal, whom would you more likely buy from—a real-estate agent who's checking himself out in every mirror in the house he's showing you, or the one who exudes self-confidence in his every step?

---

- **If you pay attention to and practice the "Three C's" of dressing** comfortably, compatibly, and confidently, your customers will respectfully pay attention to your message.
- **Every industry or profession has some kind of "dress code."** Follow it, but don't lose yourself in the process.
- Here's a short list of fashion do's and don'ts from my dressing room for you women. Borrow them if you'd like, but remember, do so only if they fit *you*.

    —Wear open-toed shoes *only* with perfectly pedicured feet. (No chipped polish allowed.)

—Wear bright-colored nail polish only with short, well-manicured fingernails.

—Carry a handbag that's user-friendly (doesn't call for digging), and make sure everything is tucked neatly inside it.

—Have a mending kit in your glove box and/or desk drawer.

—Wear only one ring on a hand at a time.

—When in doubt, wear black after five.

—Stay away from pleats. They're too schoolgirlish and don't do much for the hips.

—Stay away from overly trendy clothes and accessories unless you're selling trendy clothes and accessories.

—A jean jacket can casualize many an outfit. Own one and experiment with it.

—A black skirt, contrasted with a white blouse and topped with a black blazer, looks simple and smart.

—Buy something new to reward yourself when you reach a sales goal.

—Buy something new to perk yourself up when you're in a sales slump.

# Chapter 5

# SET THE STAGE

I f the first component of putting your best foot forward is your dress, the second is keeping your work environment professional and inviting. It shows customers that you're competent and that you care.

Whether you work from a counter, a car, a cubicle, or a corner office, doing business in an environment that's clean, functional, fully supplied, and organized is a good way to make a lasting impression—and increase your chances of making the sale.

Why is this important? First, if you show a customer—even indirectly—that you don't take care of your own environment, they're less likely to trust you to take care of them.

Second, when a customer is buying from you, your work environment is theirs, too.

Take our rest rooms in my dealerships. Since customers also use them, I consider them to be community property. If I don't take the opportunity to present clean rest rooms, I'm in effect telling my customers that I don't care about them. The reverse is also true: If I *do* make sure our rest rooms are immaculate, I'm showing my customers that I *do* care.

You see, I think the "showrooms" in my car dealerships are *all* of the rooms, which are shared with our customers, not just the rooms where bright, shiny, new-smelling cars are displayed.

All of us—in some way or another—carry out our lives in a showroom. In fact, I think of it as though we're all really in "show business." You're a star in your own life. And as long as you're breathing, you'll have critics. Your actions always have the potential to be held for or against you. (More about this in later chapters.)

There are lots of little ways to create a positive image in every area of your life. I probably should admit here that there are times I carry it to silly extremes.

My two-day-per-week housekeeper has been with me for more than a decade. Nevertheless, I try to make sure I "tidy up" before she comes, for fear she'll think I'm messy.

I nipped at my husband the other day because he sampled a cookie from the tray arranged for our company that evening. Of course, he didn't know that he should have taken one from the cookie sheet.

Whether it's cleaning up before the maid arrives or putting out perfectly arranged cookies for your guests, the premise is the same: Your "stage" is wherever you are.

## 5.1   Keep Your Stage Clean

In my professional life, my stage is my dealerships, places where I get to show my customers that I care about them. I start by making sure they are clean and sanitary. I have systems in place to ensure that the cleanliness (and general good condition) of my car dealerships is maintained.

I use internal inspectors in rotating teams of three who are accountable and empowered to make changes.

Though we make use of many outside contractors (e.g., landscapers, window washers, and a janitorial service), I believe that you get more from what you inspect than what you expect. So one day each week, four teams of three employees (including one member of management) inspect everything from the light fixtures to the flower beds. Each team literally walks their assigned area and takes note of its condition.

These internal inspectors give immediate attention to any equipment in less-than-perfect working order. For example, a sink that drips, a door that won't close properly, or a cracked mirror—all of which speak of neglect—is repaired as soon as it's discovered. (Each team of inspectors has access to our maintenance fund so they can take action as soon as a problem is found.)

If an upgrade of some sort falls outside the budget, the senior person on the team brings the team's findings and recommendations to a weekly management meeting, where we decide whether or not the proposed changes make good business sense. (Can we really afford a new fence around our property, or will some shrubbery take care of the problem for now?)

I may have the lead role, but at Love Chrysler, we're all players sharing a common mission to please our audience.

Our system seems to work: A team of high-standard inspectors from the DaimlerChrysler Corporation out of Detroit consistently rates the cleanliness of our dealerships "5 Star," the highest in the industry. That's a nice accolade, but what's more important is what our customers think. I have realized fantastic gains by preparing the stage for my toughest critics—my customers.

I received one such review just recently. A couple came in to shop for a minivan. The sales rep, trying to overcome the wife's objection to the color of the "otherwise perfect" model, asked the couple if they'd be willing to take one more look at it in "better light."

They agreed to do so, but first the wife went to the ladies' room. Upon her return, she complimented the salesperson on the rest room's condition.

A bit later, as they stood outside taking one last look at the van, the wife looked at her husband and said, "I like the color more now than I did before."

"Did the better lighting make the difference?" he asked.

"Yes, and so did the impressive ladies' room," she responded.

Once I've got the basics (like cleanliness and functionality) down, I enjoy coming up with additional displays that say to a customer, "You're important to us." Customers have enormous appreciation for small gestures of caring. And there's no better opportunity to serve these gestures up than in customer areas. I employ interesting artwork, fresh potpourri, fresh flowers, *current* reading material, comfortable homey furnishings, and a friendly greeter to help make my customers feel at home. I wouldn't offer guests coming to my home any less, and my customers *are* my guests.

Recognizing, as I mentioned before, that a block of my clientele is repeat business, I also frequently change the decor in the customer areas. I have a lot of fun doing it. (One of my biggest decorating hits was a 1950s motif in the customer lounge of my service department.)

And while we're on the subject of decor, I make it work in a way that not only impresses people but influences them as well. Take mirrors, for example. We've all heard how they make a room appear larger. But that's not all they do. If they're positioned in such a way that the person you're communicating with is faced with their own reflection, you'll discover your customer becomes easier to deal with. It can be like breaking down walls. I'm convinced that when people see themselves, they actually become nicer.

In my office, I have a large ornate mirror behind me, so when someone's on the other side of my desk, they're looking not only at me but also at themselves. I've seen it soften even the most intimidating of personalities.

It's a rare person who enjoys looking at himself or herself when they're complaining or being stubborn. Let's face it: No one looks their best in such a state.

Another means I use to break down walls is to arrange furniture in such a way that I always give my customers "space." If they want to stand and stretch or walk around during a negotiation, they can. In my experience, when someone is locked into a certain position mentally, if they're afforded the opportunity to get up and bend or stretch, their mental state as well as their bodies become more flexible.

In fact, I provide myself the same space. In writing this book, I find that whenever I get "writer's block," staring at my computer, it can stir my creativity just to get up, stretch, and walk around.

I recognize that you may not be as free to perform creative experiments with or make costly changes to your work areas. However, *everyone* can do the basics.

I am reminded here of the doctor's office I visited that had dead plants in the waiting room. You can imagine how long I remained a patient. (If they can't keep their plants alive, are they qualified to treat me?) When the receptionist witnessed me pouring water from my water bottle into one of the planters, she stopped me. "The doctor's wife tends to the plants. They're off-limits to us." I couldn't believe it. This poor gal felt so restricted in her job that she couldn't even water a dying plant.

There is a tendency to throw up your hands when you're faced with sharing customer areas with colleagues, landlords, or business owners who don't care.

A friend of mine in real estate, who describes herself as an independent agent, has just such a dilemma. She pays rent to the broker she represents, who also owns the building. "He doesn't care about the place. It's embarrassing when I have to bring clients in," she said.

As tough (and unfair) as it may sound, anytime your customers are exposed to an area via your invitation, *you* are responsible for its condition. I promise you, your customers are evaluating you based on your workplace's condition. Perhaps you're able to negotiate your lease or compensation in consideration of caretaking you give the place. But with or without it, the onus falls on you. You *personally* will reap the benefits of a well-manicured customer area, and you *personally* will suffer the sanctions sure to come with neglect. Remember, in your customer's mind, he or she is thinking, "If they neglect themselves, they'll probably neglect me, too."

A professional hairstylist I do business with uses the same approach to take care of the salon he leases space from. One day, I noticed that many of the magazines in the customer waiting area had subscription labels with his name on them. When I asked him about them, he said, "You're the third customer to notice that today. I buy the subscriptions because I care about you."

Maybe you won't be noticed for your own caring gesture, but I promise that people will notice if you don't make the effort.

I'm not suggesting that you are responsible for replacing the leaky roof that drips over your workstation. But it is up to you to work with the owner or a manager to try to get it fixed. At the very least, arrange the furniture in such a way that best hides the bucket. If your working environment is so run-down that even your most creative efforts won't cover up its faults, it's more than likely time to move on.

## 5.2   Be Organized

Even the most creative mind can be stifled when it's cluttered and disorganized.

Not only does disorganization sabotage our ability to be creative, it also consumes our energy. If I'm frantically searching for my car keys five times a day, I'm not going to be able to give my all to other activities. Running around in circles is no way to get anywhere.

Disorganization also causes us to miss opportunities if it results in having important tools where we can't access them. In sales, you don't have time to research or look for information to make your point. You have to be ready.

In my car dealerships, I encourage (almost insist) that my salespeople have the phone numbers to all the local credit unions and banks on their speed dial. That's important, because often in a salesperson's office a customer needs to learn how much money they owe on their trade-in. That figure plays into the calculation of how much of their trade-in value can be applied to their payment on their new car. When a customer says they have to obtain their "payoff" from their bank or credit union before they can make any decisions about the new car, the salesperson phones for them right there. If a salesperson has to roam around to look for a phone book or even look up a phone number, it interrupts the customer's mood to buy and the general flow of things.

In my business, we can't afford unnecessary delays. They cause customers to leave the premises—to go home and "think about it"—or to go shop at a competitor's. Good organization helps to prevent premature good-byes.

And in today's world, with all of its competing priorities, disorganization can lead to all kinds of mismanagement. We begin to lose track of what's important. Worry preempts planning, and it's not long before we feel as if our lives are spinning out of control. Disorganization is at the heart of too many failed businesses and botched sales.

The flip side of this is that being organized not only makes you *do good*, it makes you *look good*. I've come to think of organization as a cosmetic. It helps me to look my best. And usually when I look my best, I do my best.

Let me use an example from the real-estate business once again. If the vehicle you're using to transport your client(s) is cluttered, you look disorganized and cluttered, sloppy. You'll be seen as someone who doesn't care enough about your business or job to bother with the details. The "hold on while I clear the seat off for you" approach reveals that you're "less than." Less than organized. Less than prepared. Less than attentive.

When the opposite is the case, and your car is not only free from interior clutter but also shiny on the exterior (weather permitting) and in good operating order (with plenty of gas), you look good. You look like a person on top of your game. You look ready.

Part of inviting orderliness into your life is about making sure you're adequately supplied (like having fuel in your tank). I paid a visit to a male investment banker not too long ago and was quite impressed with how hospitably he greeted me. But fifteen minutes into his presentation, I asked a question that caused him to ask me to move next door. "We're going to borrow Bonnie's office because my computer doesn't have the software I need to answer your question." At that point, I felt as if I would rather be doing business with Bonnie.

In sales, as in life, customers associate preparedness with competence. When they think they've placed themselves in competent hands, the tension of buying is eased. And I would much rather present the benefits of my product or service to a relaxed potential customer than to one who's ill at ease.

When you have all the tools at your fingertips necessary to execute the sale, you're projecting yourself as someone who's competent, someone who's a pro. If you have to ask your customer to hang on while you gather supplies or information, or to otherwise organize yourself, you're inviting skepticism.

I recently witnessed such an incident involving one of my own salesmen. "Take a look at this while I try to find a credit application," the salesman suggested to his customer, handing her a magazine. This seemingly innocent attempt to occupy a customer by putting her in a "holding pattern" separated him from the customer in more ways than one. His potential customer hadn't come to our dealership to read magazines! The misstep, while not lethal (he went on to make the sale), cost everyone time, and it may have cost the salesman future referrals. Think about it. Would you want to be under the care of a surgeon who had to give you extra anesthesia while the nurses ran around the hospital looking for the right scalpel?

Organization is a mark of a true professional. I "invite" it into my career at every opportunity. In fact, if I'm upset or in a bad mood, organizing some small corner of my life actually serves to motivate me: updating an address book, reconciling an expense account, clutter-busting a credenza. Once again, I feel in control of my life; it gives me just the inspiration I need to get out of the doldrums.

Organization can not only help you to do good and to look good, it can help you *feel* good.

One last point. I'd be remiss if I didn't pass on a tip that's helped me to *stay* organized. Mail—whether it's faxed, postal, or electronic—as well as phone messages, newspapers, and other periodicals, are a source of clutter on many a desk and in many a workplace. By taking care of them decisively, I head off the chaos these communications can cause. When confronted with a piece of paper, I either save it (filed away for possible future use), act on it, label it (for someone else to act on), or exterminate it the moment it comes in.

If it helps, remember the four possible responses to any piece of paper—S-A-L-E: *S*ave, *A*ct, *L*abel, *E*xterminate. Use this acronym. It works.

But whatever systems you use, don't lose sight of the big picture: Organization is a means of becoming more effective. It helps you to keep useful tools within reach. And it helps you look like a winner.

- **Life is "show time." Your environment is your stage.** Prepare customer areas as you would your home if you were awaiting special company.
- **Good organization impresses.** It helps you to win people over.
- **Have the tools of your trade at your fingertips.** You may not be able to control the quantity of time you spend with your customers, but you *can* control the quality.

# Chapter 6

# MAKING A GOOD FIRST IMPRESSION LAST

Making a good first impression is usually pretty easy once you've subscribed to the notion that dressing appropriately and having a clean and orderly work environment are part of your daily business life. But you need to remember that the old saw about a first impression being a lasting one is *not* the case when it comes to sales. (And again, sales covers a lot of territory. Public relations, human relations, marketing, politics, law, and other fields are pure sales professions.)

In all of these worlds, you can't count on your first impression to carry you forever. In our world, the operating motto is more like "What have you done for me lately?" Even if a customer gives your "meet-and-greet" an A+, there is no guarantee you are going to make the sale. It may prevent you from blowing one, but think of everything we have talked about up until now as your starting point.

Obviously, after you have made a solid first impression, your product knowledge and ability to solve the customer's problem come into play, but there is one important factor that people tend to overlook, and that is genuinely caring about the people you are trying to help.

It begins by remembering their names. Remembering names is something that has never come easy to me. I've heard all the advice (repeat the name right away, make an immediate association, ask how it's spelled, etc.) and have employed them with some success. If you're naturally good at it, congratulations. If you're not, do as I do and keep on trying.

I know that remembering a customer's name is important. You do, too. But I submit: Having them remember yours is what *really* makes a good impression last.

Admittedly, we all want to keep our good name in the forefront of the minds of our sales prospects. That's why there's big business in the production and distribution of giveaways that tout the names of people and businesses. Baseball caps, refrigerator magnets, pens, pocket calendars, golf tees—the list of "stuff" goes on. But sustaining a good reputation takes more than stamping your name on some cheesy giveaway. As syrupy as it may sound, it matters more about what comes from your heart.

## 6.1    Engaging Your Heart

When I was selling, I used a fairly crude system of storing the details about my sales prospects' lives, as well as those of customers I had already sold a car to. (This is where getting to know your customer is invaluable. More about this in later chapters.) I would pull out an old-fashioned index card file box each time I followed up with any of them by telephone.

This box enabled me to refer to personal aspects of the customers' lives in my conversations with them. Effectively, I had talking points, ways to show them I remembered them and that I cared. I might ask, "How was your birthday?" or "Did your daughter recover from her measles?" or "How was your vacation in Cancún?" Customers generally appreciated the personal interest I took in their lives. My box system took time, organization, and a conscientious effort, and it worked fairly well. But I always felt I could do better.

What was missing, I would come to realize, is that my system engaged every fiber of my being except my heart.

Making a lasting good impression is a natural when your actions are ignited by your passion. And our creativity flows most freely when our hearts are "in the right place."

When I realized this, I continued to make deposits into my data bank of information, but I started using it more selectively and not matter-of-factly or routinely. I reallotted my time in such a way that I responded to personal information about my customers and their families only when I had an emotional interest or concern.

For example, if I learned that a woman was facing an impending divorce, I marked the date on my calendar and followed up with a "hang in there" call. If I learned that a family had just placed a loved one in a nursing home, I sent flowers to the person responsible for making that difficult decision and attached a card that read something like, "You are a lovely, loving lady." The last day of school, I made sure customers who had identified themselves as teachers received "You did it!" cards from me.

The by-product of my more personally engaged "rah-rahs," assurances, and congratulations catapulted my sales career in a way I never could have expected or dreamed. I was blessed with business I didn't even know was out there! People would come in asking for me, saying things like (I still remember them vividly), "You went to see our cousin in the hospital after she was diagnosed with cancer" or "A neighbor told us how you sent her a cheer-up card after her daughter's wedding."

What this taught me is that we really do live in a small, connected world. And that people helping people is the most powerful force not only in sales, but also in our universe.

I've come to realize that when I follow my heart in my "follow-up" with customers, I seem to get back ten times whatever I give.

This same "follow-up" tenet also works when you've botched a first impression. Let me give you an example:

A new fellow director of a state bureau for consumer rights attended her first board meeting and left all of us wondering about her future service and contributions to the organization. It was obvious that she hadn't familiarized herself with the agenda or anything else relative to the group or the meeting. She sat through the entire session quite clueless.

One month later, when the next meeting rolled around, she was there early, greeting everyone as they came in. Off to the side, she asked the chairman for permission to address all of the members before the meeting was called to order. "I just wanted to tell all of you that I am appropriately embarrassed by my inability to contribute at last month's meeting. I look forward to showing you just how exceptional that was for me." Neither I nor any of the other board members got to know the reasons why she wasn't prepared at the last meeting, but given the sincerity of her comments, it didn't matter. She was speaking from her heart when she let us know that she was aware of—and claimed responsibility for—her inappropriate behavior. We were all left with the sense that she was not likely to repeat the poor performance. And she never did.

Heartfelt sincerity goes a long way toward making people like you.

## 6.2   Let Your Emotions Work for You

We all want to be liked. But I believe it's also good to show or tell the other person *you* like *them*. Personally, I love to be around people who I think like me. They help me to feel good about myself. So it's quite natural to have a good impression of people who you believe have a good first impression of you. That's why I love Whoopi Goldberg.

As an honoree at a luncheon in New York City, I was seated next to the Oscar winner and comedienne, who was the guest speaker. During lunch, as we were chatting, out of the blue she laughed at something I said and exclaimed, "I like you!"

By telling me that, she moved way up on my list of favorite celebrities.

You need not be a movie star to benefit from creating a fan base for yourself. Making a good first impression last—or reversing a bad one—is all about showing people that you truly care about them *and* that you like them. The path to becoming influential is paved by your ability and willingness to show your emotional side. And for a woman, that should be a natural!

- **Make a good impression last.** Follow up with prospects and customers.
- **Listen to your heart.** It doesn't lie to you. Others will see the honesty in your deeds.
- **Be emotionally engaged with your customer.** It takes courage, but it builds trust.

# Chapter 7

# IT'S ABOUT TIME

## 7.1 Always Show Up on Time

Woody Allen said, "Ninety percent of success is showing up." I would add that the other 10 percent involves showing up *on time.*

In today's fast-track world, being "fashionably late" is quickly going out of style.

Tardiness is like smoking. They're both bad habits that, when stopped, can have an almost immediate, positive impact. To stop smoking is one of the greatest things you can do to improve your health. Adopting a "no more tardiness" resolution is the single greatest behavioral change you can make to improve your wealth.

Even better than being on time is being early.

At 7 A.M., the hustle and bustle inside a car dealership service department is constant. You always have customers eager to get on with their day, fumbling with their coffee cups, briefcases, tote bags, and cell phones as they drop off their cars for service. And typically during this heavy-traffic time, the sales department is not yet open.

As a salesperson, I saw and seized an obvious opportunity to be helpful by getting to work early. Greeting people waiting around for a shuttle van or rental car, I offered customers an alternate (quicker) mode of getting to work. I chauffeured them. By my getting to work early, I helped them not to be late.

And I discovered that by solving their first problem of the day, they opened up to me, inviting me into their lives to solve their transportation needs. Many of them came to the realization that a *new* source of transportation was in order: "I think I might be better off making payments on a new car than to continue to spend money fixing this one. Maybe I should set up a time to come talk to you."

It was all about time—using mine to save theirs.

Department stores use this "invest your time to save your customers time" philosophy in their marketing, as well. Think about the way they display fragrance sets for Mother's Day. They keep a good supply on hand already gift-wrapped. It saves the buyer time not having to run around to a gift-wrapping department or to another store to purchase wrapping paper, not to mention the time it takes to do the wrapping. Bottom line: It makes the purchase so much easier and more inviting.

If being on time is good, and being early is even better, why are so many people notorious for being late? An executive I once worked with proudly proclaimed he was intentionally five minutes late for meetings in consideration of the other person's time. "The people I deal with are very busy, and they seem to welcome the extra five minutes my tardiness gives them," he told me. Though his argument might on the surface seem to make sense, I don't recommend it. While it's true that I have on occasion welcomed an appointment being slightly late, it's risky. It's best to assume that the person you're calling on has an air-tight schedule. Having to kick off a sales meeting with an apology is just bad business. Rather than starting from neutral ground, you have a deficit to make up—not a winning strategy.

What do you do on that rare occasion when you are late?

Apologize—cleanly and crisply. Don't eat up more of your customer's time belaboring excuses. "I'm sorry I'm a bit late. I won't waste any more of your time with my excuses." That's enough. When you offer excuses, you position yourself in a bad light. If, for example, you say "I couldn't get a taxi," your prospect hears "poor planner." If you say "I got hung up with a long-winded caller," your prospect may conclude that you are not in control.

Time is one of the ways in which we're truly all created equal. You and your customer have exactly the same amount of time in each day.

That's why tardiness conveys a tone of arrogance, a disregard for your customer's time. ("My time's more important than yours.") *Make a positive impression by never being late.*

I want my customers to notice that not only am I on time, but that I've been waiting for them. That creates a powerful impression. It makes them feel special.

I first learned this valuable business lesson from my grand-mother. When I go to visit her—even today when she is in her nineties—she greets me at the front door. I never have to knock. And even before I have the chance to take off my coat, she's handing me my favorite beverage poured into a glass, which she's made extra cold by keeping it in the freezer. She gives life to the impression that she waits on her guests.

I've carried her approach into my business dealings. On hot Texas days, I offer complimentary chilled bottles of spring water at our dealerships. (They're much more inviting than drinking fountains or big dispensers with white, cone-shaped mini-cups that offer you but one awkward swig.) If a customer is coming in to look at a particular car, my salespersons make sure it's pulled up front, buffed, and full of gas. Our customers are treated like my grandmother's visitors. We've been waiting for them. We've been looking forward to their arrival.

The manager of one of my favorite local restaurants uses what I think of as the "we've been waiting for you" practice, as well. When we arrive for our reservation, she not only has our table waiting, she's prepared in such a way that makes us feel welcome. She'll have our favorite merlot "breathing" at our table in anticipation of our arrival. While it might seem like a bit of a risk to make such an assumption (What if we wanted something different that night?), her gesture has more than paid off.

A real-estate agent who arrives for a "property showing" early enough to open the blinds, turn on the lights, and start the air conditioner or heater has a huge advantage over one who arrives late and has to struggle with the lockbox. Even if the property isn't the right one, I can promise that the agent who arrives early to prepare for and await the client has shown she *is* the right agent for them.

In the same way, if you're awaiting an appointment, let your customers sense that you have been waiting for them when they walk in. It's a mark of your respect for them. Don't hide it.

Have their file in front of you. Be familiar with it. Have your pencil sharpened, necessary forms within easy reach, paper in your adding machine, your computer turned on, the coffee hot, and a coaster within easy reach.

If you're the one doing the calling, use the rest room ahead of time. Have your tote or briefcase organized in such a way that you reach into it only once for any presentation materials.

I witnessed one job applicant lose out in the interview process because she didn't heed this advice. She had just interviewed with my business manager. She smiled at me as she passed by on her way out of the administrative office. I commented to our business manager that I had been impressed with the candidate's exit.

"Well, unfortunately, her entrance left something to be desired," the manager told me. "She arrived ten minutes late, out of breath, and the first thing she said was 'Where's the ladies' room?'"

So be punctual and efficient out of respect for your customer's time. Show them with every gesture and detail that you've been looking forward to their visit.

## 7.2    Use an Appointment System

I make appointments for almost everything I do in my life. In doing so, I'm seen by others as a person who's got her act together. (I even make appointments for quiet time by myself. Having a little time to myself renews my peace of mind and brings order to my life.)

In any kind of sales transaction, getting your customer or client to agree to an appointment, even if you have all the time in the world, accomplishes two things. It conveys an image of competence. It also helps to promote a commitment on the part of the customer.

One of my girlfriends used this concept with me not long ago when she called to invite me to come see her new office.

"I'll see how my morning goes. I'll call you later," I told her.

"How about four-thirty? We can christen my new office with my new wineglasses," she said temptingly.

"Okay. I'll be there," I said. It was more than the idea of sharing a late-afternoon glass of wine with my friend that elicited the commitment I gave her. It was the exact time she proposed. I became more committed to dropping by because she converted a vague invitation into an exact request.

I once had a sales manager question my attempt to set an exact time. He overheard me asking a sales prospect on the phone if six o'clock or six-thirty would be better for them. "You're on shift until nine tonight," the sales manager said. "Why'd you pin that customer down to an exact time when you had more flexibility?" (He would rather have heard me simply tell the customer that I would be available until closing time.)

I explained that I "pinned them down" the way that I did because it made it more likely that they'd show up. It also created the impression that my time was in demand. And before long, it was!

I've also learned to make appointments to call a customer back when I'm too harried to give them my undivided attention at the moment of their call. For example, if I don't have the information someone is requesting at my fingertips, or even if I just need time to think about how I want to handle the call, I'll ask the caller, "Can we set up a time when I can get back with you so I can double-check our information?" It's not a stall tactic—I believe it is in the best interest of my caller to have my undivided attention. (One caution: If you use this, you'd better do all your prep work before you call back.)

Whether to create a good image or to carve out the time to prep for the call, the best of the best always work by appointment. It's true in almost every profession. Lawyers who hang around waiting for walk-ins are either just right out of law school or probably not very good. Women brag about having their hair done by the stylist who is booked four weeks in advance. The best restaurants take reservations weeks ahead of time.

Think about it—it's human nature to desire that which is scarce. Gold and diamonds are precious because there's a limited supply. In a world of deadlines and expirations, I truly believe we make ourselves more valuable in the minds of our customers when we promote appointments.

I overheard my secretary (one of my best promoters) on the phone the other day telling the caller that I had "very few travel dates open for the year." When I asked her what that was all about, she explained that the caller was inquiring about my availability for speaking at a conference that was in the planning process. By presenting my availability as something that was limited (a truth), she encouraged the caller to act quickly and decisively. They called back the same day and booked me.

Everyone will delay making a decision when there's no motivation to do so. It gives them time to gather more information, to be more certain. None of us likes to make decisions in the face of uncertainty. That's why we resist making commitments if we don't have to. But to take control of your life, you've got to be able to ask for commitments. And converting "I can do this anytime" to "I can do this at this time" is a good place to start.

Making an appointment with yourself (for example, "I won't do any work between three and four today") serves a different purpose. Setting aside that kind of appointment is about creating order in your life. The panic of "Oh my goodness, I didn't get around to calling so-and-so" is a lot less likely to occur if you set aside a regular time for self-organization. It helps you to stay on track.

In sales, and in life for that matter, we can get so busy reacting that we don't have time to be proactive. That's why it's so important to call time-outs. Only then can we reflect and plan.

You need to make time to be alone for the purpose of setting priorities both in your own mind and on paper. I use the acronym L-I-S-T-S to remind myself of its importance: *Life's Information, Sorted, Triggers Sales.*

Use whatever technology you're comfortable with—pencil and paper, Palm Pilot, laptop, desktop computer—the idea is the same. Think of prioritizing and organizing your life. Make sure you do it at a time when you're not doing anything else. This is hard for many of us as we've become such multitaskers. But it's best to concentrate on this task fully and prioritize everything that you need to do.

## 7.3  Good Timing Is Everything

When I was a kid, if my mom was wearing curlers, I knew better than to ask her for anything. Maybe they gave her a headache, or maybe she just felt ugly wearing them, but curlers to me meant "Better wait till later."

We all remember that if we wanted our parents to let us do something or go somewhere, good timing was crucial. As kids, we were pretty astute at picking up signals about our parents' moods. Yet, in the professional sales world, too often we suffer from amnesia. Timing is everything!

It might seem that a section on good timing fits better in a discussion about negotiation than on time management. (In later chapters, I have plenty to say about the art of good timing when it comes to negotiating.) After all, bad timing can derail a sales process so thoroughly that the aftermath resembles something akin to a train wreck.

But that's precisely why bad timing is the enemy of good time management. When we're forced to stop and pick up pieces from a shattered customer relationship, we're not moving forward very fast.

I recently witnessed a man giving an airline ticket agent his credit card to cover the cost of an airline box. His bag was overweight according to the airline's new luggage policy, and the ticket agent told him he would need to take some of his belongings out of his suitcase and place them in the box she provided. The passenger tried to persuade the agent to change her mind, saying that it was going to be a tremendous inconvenience for him to have to split the contents of his luggage. Considering other points he made—that their revised policy had just taken effect, and that he was also one of their frequent fliers—the agent initially gave in to his plea.

"Just remember our policy next time you fly with us," she said.

But instead of saying thank you, the traveler ill-advisedly said: "Your so-called weight policy would have me actually transporting more weight. I'd be shipping the box, in addition to all my stuff. It's illogical." His timing couldn't have been worse.

Without saying a word, she reversed course and proceeded to process his credit card and hand him the box.

Obviously, he would have been better off making his argument later by writing a letter to customer service. Would it have made a difference? Who knows. But what we know for sure is that his timing cost him.

Good timing is about more than just knowing when to say what. It's also critical to know when *not* to say something.

In car sales, a good salesperson knows not to discuss trade-in values, payment plans, and the like during a demonstration drive—even when asked about them. It's not a matter of withholding the information, but rather of *holding* the information— for later—in order to allow the customer to get the full benefit of the drive.

Often a customer asked during the test drive, "How much do you think my trade-in is worth?"

"Allow me to answer that for you later, when we're in my office," I would reply.

First, I didn't want something to interfere with their falling in love with the car. Not only did I want them paying full attention to the road and the features of the new car, but later I would want their undivided attention as I presented information pertinent to the transaction.

Do customers object to this? No. In fact, I discovered that deferring a subject until later so that it can be properly discussed is not only okay with most customers, it is appreciated. It gives them a preview of what is ahead in the sales process— something we talked about earlier.

Deferring an answer also makes you more needed by the customer. Effectively, you've invited them to stay with you. What they're asking for is coming up. (Of course, you can't be impolite about it. For example, if my response had been, "You'll get that information when I'm ready to give it to you," the customer would have probably made a U-turn and returned to the lot.)

Speaking of test drives and poor timing, I've actually had salesmen tell me that they use the test drive to probe customers about their creditworthiness, price expectations, or readiness to buy. That, to me, is the equivalent of asking a first date what her interest is in having children. It's inappropriate, if not plain offensive.

## BUYING SIGNS

A buying sign is a green light, a signal that the customer is ready to strike a deal or make a purchase. Salespeople ignore such signals at their peril. This is the time to close the deal.

Here are a few examples of buying signs:

- "Wouldn't it be serendipitous if I bought my second home on another street named after a flower," a client tells a real-estate agent.
- "This necklace would look nice on my wife," a customer tells a jeweler. That's a clear buying sign—a sign that the time is now to confirm his choice and close the transaction.
- "I'm glad we cleaned out the garage Sunday," a wife tells her husband in the presence of a car salesman as they look over the new cars. That's a buying sign—a sign that they are ready to go ahead with the purchase of a new car.
- "I'm not normally inclined to make exceptions to our vacation policy," a supervisor tells an employee. That's a buying

sign—a sign that the time is now to say, "I appreciate your making an exception for me."

Virtually any time a sales prospect says something that suggests they've taken mental ownership of a product or an idea, the time is right for you to take it to the next step and move toward closing the sale (something we talk about more later).

Very seldom will a customer say, "I'll take it" or "Where can I pay for this?" Whenever you are selling, whether at work or in life, failure to recognize a buying sign can cause unnecessary delays in the closing process—and missed sales.

It's soooo frustrating to look back and realize that a sales opportunity was missed. "I wasted so much of my time and didn't get the sale" becomes your mind-set. But the reality of it is that you also wasted your customer's time.

---

- **Always show up on time.** Your customers are important. And to make sure they feel that way—whether you're calling on them or they're calling on you—give them the impression that you've been waiting to see them.

- **Use an appointment system.** It creates the impression that your time is valuable in the eyes of the customer and shows them that you value theirs, too.

- **Use good timing.** Hold on to information or questions until the right time. Be ready to respond when your customer reveals "buying signs."

# Chapter 8

# REFLECTED GLORY: USING OTHER PEOPLE'S ASSETS TO STRENGTHEN YOURS

My grandfather used to tell me, "Show me who your friends are and I'll tell you what *you* are." Of course, he was trying to persuade me to stay away from "the wrong people" in order to preserve my reputation. It was good advice. But I have taken my grandfather's premise a bit further. I try to surround myself with people who will *enhance* my reputation.

I am not talking about taking advantage of someone else's name or accomplishments in order to seem more important than you are. But I do make it a point to associate with people who are accomplished, interesting, who challenge me, and who I feel are "good" people. And I'm not shy about drawing on these relationships when necessary.

Let me give you a brief example involving my husband. I serve on an advertising board that creates and places ads for Chrysler car dealerships (including my own). In the beginning,

as the only female car dealer on the Texas council, it was a challenge trying to fit in. The guys were nice enough, but my ideas
and suggestions were received as if they were being made by an
alien from another planet.

I kept trying, but time and time again I found no one listening to my ideas.

One day, after returning home after another meeting where I
wasn't heard, I shared my frustration with my husband, Tim.
"Our meeting in the morning was so rushed that I didn't have
time to make my points," I told him. "They were all in a hurry
to make their one o'clock tee time." (The meeting was held, as
usual, at a beautiful golf resort.)

"They probably continue the meeting on the golf course,"
Tim said. Then it hit me! He was right. After the golf outing,
during which I would go to the spa, we would typically all
meet for dinner. While we were eating, I was always amazed at
how solidly in sync they were about any upcoming business
plan. The realization that the real meeting was being conducted
on the golf course caused me to feel even more out of it than
I had felt earlier in the day. This couldn't continue. *I* needed
a plan.

Now, my husband's a very good (and very passionate) golfer.
And so I asked him to accompany me to the next month's
meeting. After all, many of my male colleagues brought their
wives. (They hung out at the spa, too.) Tim didn't have to be
asked twice.

This time when we all met for dinner, the atmosphere was
different. Tim's heroics on the golf course had made me—by
extension—one of them. Because they were awed by my husband's play, they began to hear *my v*oice differently.

Did I use my husband? Yes, although it was with his full understanding and cooperation. (I think it's safe to say he got something out of it, too. You don't have to ask Tim twice to play golf, especially at a topflight, challenging course.)

I am not suggesting that you "use" people in a way that's deceitful or hurtful. But your association with others can be beneficial (or harmful) to the advancement of your cause.

Like it or not, we're judged by the company we keep. It is just a fact. I have found that when I accept—and even employ—this concept, rather than deny or resist it, I am able to wield more influence over others and exert more power to shape my own life.

Let me give you another example; it involves my role as building campaign chairperson for the local chapter of The Women's Shelter. To meet my self-imposed stretch goal of raising $500,000 one year, I knew that I needed to get the word out. And given the amount of money I needed to raise, that meant getting my message on radio and TV. I needed a media partner to get the job done, because we didn't have any money to advertise.

And so I decided to draw on my own purchasing power to start the process. As the owner of a number of dealerships, I'm a pretty healthy advertiser. I set up a lunch meeting with one of the network's local television executives and asked them for their help. I managed to get a "We'll take a look at all of our other public service commitments and get back with you." Then I waited. And waited. Finally, I decided that I would have to make the next move. But in order to avoid a replay of my first presentation, I knew that I needed something more.

The "more" that I decided on was connecting my important project (and myself) with important people. I called the mayor and the chief of police. Knowing that it would benefit them politically (not to mention the fact that they're both good people with strong social consciences) to participate in this worthwhile cause, I organized another lunch meeting with the local station. The lure: They would have face-to-face time with two of the city's most powerful officials.

At the meeting, the chief of police told the TV executives horror stories of how women and children were sometimes turned away from the shelter in the middle of the night because there was no room for them. They listened as the mayor told them that I had the full support of her office in whatever I needed for this project. And they listened as I explained that the project would position them as a great friend to the community; I made it clear I was prepared to step up to the plate in every way—coming up with the creative stuff, staff, and time, and paying to produce the spots, in order to make the public service announcements happen.

In the end, we formed a great partnership and raised the money faster than I could have hoped. The chief of police, mayor, and network executives were all present for both the ground breaking and the ribbon cutting (which took place less than a year later).

In effect, what I had managed to do was to turn up the volume of my own voice by recruiting other people to chime in. It's something I've found that women are good at. Women inherently reach out to others. (When was the last time you saw a man asking for directions?) So it's a stratagem that comes easier for us women. But men can learn it, too.

Not only are women more likely to ask for assistance with life's heavy lifting, we're more likely to ask someone how to do something in the first place. (Most men I know don't even like to read instructions.)

## 8.1    Teach Me, Teach Me

If you want to be successful, it's vital that you create and nurture relationships with others. It's one of the key ways we learn in life and in our careers. We all owe it to ourselves. But it can happen only when you reach out to others (often outside of your comfort zone) and make yourself a student or apprentice. (Another variation of my grandfather's saying is "Show me who your friends are and I'll tell you what *you're going to become*.")

When I started selling, I couldn't help but notice that the salesmen would often congregate at an outside corner of the showroom, waiting for customers to drive up. I found the conversations on "lookout point," as I referred to it, to be something less than stimulating. (On any given day, they might range from complaints about management to complaints about women. And while they all talked about sports, the single guys liked to talk about another kind of "scoring.")

During my downtime, I opted to hang out in the finance office. I found it abuzz with all kinds of activity and learning opportunities. Given the sheer volume of paperwork, the finance manager was always in need of a helping hand. I volunteered, and was a great help. Well, most of the time. My ambition sometimes led to mistakes. (Like the time I "forgot" to collect a $1,000 down payment from a customer. When I called them up hoping to appeal to their sense of honesty, they responded, "Sorry, but you *did* give us a receipt." It's true; I had. I didn't have a leg to stand on. I had to pay up. The check I wrote to the dealership still stings.)

But my lessons paid off. Within two years, I became a finance manager at another dealership. That seemingly small decision to "hang out" with the finance manager—instead of my peers at the "point"—was a stepping-stone in my success.

Learning. I love it. It might be something as simple and straightforward as a new trick on the computer or a better way to keep my files organized. I have noticed over the years that I am supremely happy when I am employing some new system or idea that I have just learned or have just been inspired to create.

It's a real boost to your self-esteem to be able to say, "I did it!" And while personal experience *is* a great teacher, how much faster and more thorough you can be by learning from someone else's trial and error. You save time and frustration.

## 8.2   Name-dropping

"Success by association" can be as simple as subtle forms of name-dropping. Even a "cold call" is warmed by dropping the right name. "Mr. Jones, I'm So-and-so, an old acquaintance of your sister, Janet." Or: "Ms. Smith, I'm So-and-so—like you, a member of Executive Women's International." Name-dropping gives the listener pause to hear the rest of your message. We've all seen it work.

But, unlike other sales stratagems, I feel compelled to offer this one with a strong warning:

**1. Those who constantly drop names to get heard eventually lose their own voice.** I knew a lady who, in almost every conversation she engaged in, talked in terms of her husband. It didn't matter whether the subject was politics, religion, or business, *her* listeners got to hear only *his* take on all of it. She came off sounding like she had no experiences or opinions of her own.

Sadly, in my industry too often the salesmen use a strategy of pointing a finger at someone else during a negotiation. "Make me out to be the bad guy," I've heard sales managers tell their salesmen. I disagreed with that strategy years ago when I first heard it, and I still do.

My strong view was cultivated in an early lesson of selling. I had an office (separated only by a glass wall) next to a nice guy who was a somewhat less-than-successful salesman. One day, as I overheard him talking to a couple, I couldn't help but register their reaction to his approach. (In about fifteen minutes of back-and-forth negotiation, he made at least a dozen references to "the manager.") Finally, the husband burst out in frustration, "Bring Mr. Blank Face in here. There's no point in us trying to deal with *you*!"

The salesman had devalued himself so much in the eyes of his customers that he lacked any expertise or authority. That's precisely the essence of this warning. When you overuse someone else's title or name, it makes you appear powerless.

**2. Someone who uses other people's names to distort a reality eventually gets found out and loses credibility.**

Before you use anyone's name, you need to know that you can. Sounds obvious, right? After all, a name is a personal belonging. You wouldn't borrow their car without their blessing. A name is no less important to someone than their car. But you'd be amazed how many times people don't ask.

Many times I have been asked to allow my name to be used in support of some worthwhile cause. But before I say yes, I'm always very careful that I'm in a position to participate in some other way as well (offering my time or money). I personally feel it would be disingenuous for me to have my name on a letter-head, thereby associating it with an organization that I am in no way involved with.

I was distressed on one occasion to see my name on the let-terhead of a local charity that had never even called me! That act discredited their otherwise worthwhile mission. (When asked about the charity, I had to tell my friends and associates that there had been an error on the part of the organization. Eventually, I asked them to stop using it.)

Using someone's name in any way that distorts the true nature of your relationship with them is just plain dishonest.

But with these important cautions out of the way, let's talk about the proper use of name-dropping. The fact is, it can be a very effective tool both in and out of the office.

Let me give you an example from a trip to Bermuda I under-took to speak at a conference. After a flight of several hours, complete with a missed connection, an aborted flight, and a lost piece of luggage, I finally arrived exhausted at my hotel.

And then things got worse.

"The hotel manager would like a word with you, Ms. Brem," the desk clerk said as I tried to check in.

Then she escorted me to the hotel manager's office, where I sat alone for five long minutes. When the manager finally entered, he was quick with his handshake and apology for the wait. He got right to the point—he told me that the hotel was "oversold." He begged my forgiveness and proceeded to unveil his plan to remedy the fiasco. "I need your cooperation only for tonight. I'll reimburse you what you paid to stay here as well as put you up at our sister hotel. I have a car and a driver standing by to take you."

When I explained to him that my conference was scheduled to begin at noon the next day (at his hotel) and that this was going to pose a considerable inconvenience, he sweetened the pot even more. "You can check in at ten in the morning. I'll have you upgraded to a suite at no extra charge. Your room will be ready if I have to clean it myself," he responded.

"Okay, let me have your business card. Show me to my driver," I said.

The next morning, I returned to the conference hotel at ten on the dot. The front desk gave me the key to my suite and I was on my way. But when I opened the door to my room, I saw the room was a mess. It had not been cleaned!

I pulled out the manager's card and went on the warpath.

First, I found a hotel maid in the hallway. I gave her an abbreviated version of what had happened up to this point, with the manager's business card as my evidence. I asked her if she could move my room up on her list and clean it next.

"Certainly. Right away," she said.

Next I went to the front desk (the clerk on duty was a different one from the day before) and asked for the manager. He wasn't available. Again I told my story, using the manager's business card to support it. The clerk shook her head in dismay, reaching for the phone to call housekeeping (they were already on it) and then into her drawer for a dinner voucher.

Granted, the hotel obviously had some organization problems. But the point here is that if I had not had the weight of the manager's business card (remember, I'm terrible with names), I don't think I would have gotten very far in my attempt to persuade the maid or the desk clerk that they needed to act with all the speed at their disposal. By dropping his name at the appropriate juncture, I was able to get all that he promised and then some. This kind of "name-dropping" can be enormously effective.

Here are a few name-dropping tips, in addition to using someone's business card as verification.

1. Mention the name of an organization (church, alma mater, club) to which you both belong to break the ice and get your message heard.
2. "I'm a friend of a friend" is a simple but effective way to introduce yourself to a person you wish to meet.
3. "Your friend is also my customer" can be a good way to gain credibility for yourself and/or your product or company, *provided* you've cleared it with your original customer.

## 8.3   Finance Your Ideas with "Other People's Money"

Sole proprietors are all but extinct in today's business world. Partnerships are ubiquitous, even where they're not apparent. The hairstylist—with his own exclusive clientele—pays rent to work under someone else's shingle. The independent real-estate agent pays a fee to have the name of a major broker stamped on her business card. Two seemingly unrelated businesspeople share office space and the services of a secretary. Many a doctor's office now operates under the name of an "association."

As a franchisee, I am linked to a parent company, Daimler-Chrysler Corporation. They design and build the cars. I sell and service them.

Though partnerships come in many shapes and sizes, they all have one thing in common. The glue that holds a partnership together is money. (Even my two sons—who now run my businesses and who love me very much—expect to be paid for their services.) If money is the glue that binds, how do you go about using someone else's money to make more?

First of all, let me say that I learned from the experts that the fastest and easiest way to get ahead *is* to use other people's money. "OPM," it's called in all the business schools. It took me a long time to come around to this position.

My well-meaning grandparents—who taught me the value of a dollar and a good work ethic—left me with the impression that "debt" was a four-letter word. And so, for the most part, I took great pride in avoiding it as a young adult. That is, until debt found me.

I can still recall the panic I felt at age thirty-two when the administrative office of the hospital called to tell me they needed me to make "arrangements" to pay for my cancer surgery (mastectomy) and hospital stay. I was floored—I hadn't left the hospital yet! (As I mentioned earlier, I had no health insurance.)

I had no choice but to call on bankers to borrow (and plead). My family's "clear title" to our car now belonged to the hospital. But my survival depended upon my accessing "other people's money."

Today, I'm thankful for that emergency. With it came great life lessons. I have framed on my office wall three canceled checks—two for $25 and one for $100—the final payments (of the $500,000 total) I made for my medical care. They remind me that what once seemed insurmountable was manageable one dollar at a time.

Obviously, I'm not proposing that you wait until you're in dire straits before you access other people's assets.

When I started feeling a desire to go out on my own and open a car dealership, I voiced my desire to small, safe audiences—close friends and relatives who always congratulated me for my ambition and gave me "you go, girl" encouragement. That was nice, but I needed *cash*. (Thanks to my medical bills, I didn't have enough money in the bank to buy a used car, let alone a new-car dealership.)

But somehow I knew that not everybody who owned a car agency wrote a check to get it. And so I decided to take my ambitious yearning to another audience. I invited a senior Chrysler executive to lunch. "How much money would I need to get started?" I asked.

He said, "Eight hundred thousand dollars."

I heard "Eight hundred billion dollars"! It was all the same to me.

Leaving that lunch, I felt rocked into reality. But the only thing bigger than the number he gave me was my belief in myself. I knew I could run my own dealership if only I could find someone to share my belief. (Someone with money.)

It had been less than five years since I had sold my first car. That was a strike against me. But rather than focus on what I didn't have, I decided to focus on what I *did* have. And what I did have was a very good (though short) track record in selling.

It was while selling a car (a few days after that unforgettable lunch) to a man who described himself as a "financial planner" that I took the next step.

Enjoying a good rapport with him, I asked him for advice about what I might do to seek financing for a new business. He suggested that I find a "venture capitalist."

I was so naive at the time that I went home and looked up

"venture capitalists" in the yellow pages of the phone book. A minor dead end. (They don't advertise.)

Luckily, I wasn't too discouraged to do what I did next. I organized evidence of my accomplishments into a folder: letters of recommendation from the bankers whom I submitted customers' credit applications to; from vendors I dealt with in the normal course of business (computer consultant, uniform supplier, media account executives, etc.); from my customers, many of whom were repeat customers (and many who said that I had helped them make a seemingly impossible dream of owning a new car come true). I included evidence of professional achievements such as my "Top Salesman of the Month" (and "Year") certificates, "Sales Manager Inner Circle Society" certificate (membership criterion: top 5 percent of Chrysler sales managers in the nation), my certificates from completing the Automatic Data Processing and Auto Finance and Insurance courses, and press clippings. I even made copies of my Super Bowl ticket stubs saved from the trip I had won from selling cars. When I finished, even *I* was impressed.

Then I mailed about twenty of these packages out to financial planners and CPAs (I *did* find them listed in the phone book) in Texas. Common sense told me that I needed to get my package to representatives of wealthy clients. To find out which twenty I should send them to, I made phone calls to learn which firms specialized in representing medical professionals. This took less spadework than it might seem. (Receptionists at CPA firms are very savvy people.)

My package included a cover letter that revealed what I was looking for and what I had to offer to the right partner. I had the résumé side of the partnership. I needed only financial backing to pair it with. The letter in my package told prospective partners that while I acknowledged the risk they would be taking was considerable, I believed their potential return was much greater. I all but guaranteed them a handsome return on their investment. I received a call within the first couple of weeks from a stranger who said, "I represent a client who might have some interest in what you're proposing. But first I'd like to meet with you."

I met with the CPA. I liked him. He liked my determination. He arranged a series of meetings where I met his client. Concerns—such as my "lack of experience in the service end of the business"—were discussed openly. I explained that I had excelled in sales because I had been extremely "service-oriented."

The meetings truly drew on my sales ability. I was able to put into action all I had learned from selling cars (including everything contained in the pages of this book). Once again, my car-selling skills proved to be transferable to another arena.

In the end, the deal was crafted in such a way that the wealthy doctor invested some money up front, with me borrowing the remainder, hundreds of thousands of dollars. We both guaranteed the loans. (I believe in the end, had he been living, my grandfather would have forgiven me.)

I suppose the rest is history. I retired my debt to my partner, interest and all, within two years.

Maybe you don't need an $800,000 business partner. Maybe you need just a small boost to take you to the next level of selling your product or service. Perhaps you need a small credit line at your local bank to allow you to stock more of the cosmetic line in the business you run from your kitchen. Maybe a friend would like to join you in your venture. With a partner, a customer base might double. Perhaps a bigger office in a better location would allow you to enhance the image of your services. Maybe you could trade your services in return for the office. The possibilities are limitless when you think in terms of partnering. To get to the next level, think in terms of borrowing (trading for) other people's assets. It's okay. Really. Providing they get something, too.

That's the measure of a good partnership. The relationship has always got to benefit both parties. The give-and-take is the yin and the yang of the trade. So whether it's reputation, name, space, time, talent, or money that you're borrowing from a partner, always make sure they're pleased with what they're getting from you in return.

- **Reflected glory.** My grandfather was right. People do judge you by the people you associate with. Keep that in mind.
- **There is nothing wrong with name-dropping . . .** provided (a) you have the blessing of the person whose name you're using, (b) you don't lose who you are in the process, and (c) you go about it honestly. Name-dropping as part of your introduction can provide instant credibility and an instant bond.
- **Debt, when used wisely, can be a good thing.** It's unusual when someone pays cash for their car or their home. Risk and benefit need to be weighed when making a car or a mortgage loan. When it comes to investing in yourself, think about taking the same approach (measuring risk and benefit) to borrow money.

# Chapter 9

# SELLING OUTSIDE YOUR "TERRITORY"

## 9.1 Life Doesn't Have an "Off" Switch

Throughout our lives, every person we interact with forms an opinion about us. It may not be a lasting one, but if we're engaged in other people's lives in any capacity, we're "on stage," whether we recognize it or not. People are judging us. Think about it. The driver who suddenly cuts in front of you with no warning, causing you to slam on your brakes, is not someone you'd want to have watch over your children. The cashier at the supermarket who never looks up at you is not someone you'd want to have over to dinner. The out-of-control mom at a Little League game is not someone you'd want to take a vacation with.

By contrast, the woman in a long rest-room line who lets a small child go before her is someone you might want to befriend. And a restaurateur who calls to arrange for the return of the designer sunglasses you left behind is someone you'd want to return a favor to. I often judge people I meet in every-day situations by their own behavior. I bet you do, too.

Here's the point: As a salesperson, you need to recognize that your actions—in *and* out of the selling arena (that is, in and outside of the place that you traditionally do business)—have the potential to work in your favor or against you. Because you never know when a potential customer is near, it's always best to assume that they are.

Carl Sewell, the country's largest luxury car dealer, is a leg-end in my business. Someone once asked Sewell if he had a code of ethics for his employees. Here it is in its entirety: If you wouldn't want your actions printed in your hometown newspa-per, or shown on the local news, don't do them.

You never know when life's cameras may be rolling. Some of our most embarrassing moments happen not only when we least expect them but in the most unlikely of places, too. One of mine came when I was vacationing thousands of miles from home.

During my first years in business, I was the sole spokesperson for my dealerships. (I have since passed this baton to my younger son, Travis.) I wanted my customers to know that I was a caring, involved, on-site owner, and I didn't feel that someone else could convey that for me. And so I became very visible in South Texas—I was all over the "tube." There were times when I worried that people might get sick of my homespun ads (and me). But the sales kept coming, and so I kept "keepin' on."

In fact, business was so good that I sponsored a well-deserved family holiday in Hawaii with my sons and a couple of close friends. One day, coming out of a busy restaurant in Hawaii, I took a dare to pose for a street sketch artist. In the spirit of the moment, I was being silly, and overexaggerated my pose as if I were a movie star (one hand behind my head and one on my hip).

Then I heard a voice: "Are you from Corpus Christi, Texas?"

"Yes, I am," I said, straightening up. The man introduced himself and his wife. They were South Texas residents also on vacation. We chatted for a few minutes, and all the while I sensed the man's wife giving me a "don't you get enough attention at home?" look. Clearly, I had not won her over.

Okay, maybe I'm being overly sensitive here. But the point remains—it truly is a small world. And there's no public place where people aren't looking.

Most of us have engaged, at some point in our lives, in "people watching." It's a great deal more common and entertaining in my book than bird-watching. It's also a great way to pass the time during airport layovers. I recently witnessed an otherwise very attractive twenty-something girl whispering with a pointed finger to her boyfriend to "check out that fat lady." Then she giggled. To me, her outward beauty quickly faded. I was certain *I'd* never hire her if she came to me for a job.

Remember, each of us is *always* on stage.

## BEWARE OF GOSSIP

People love to hear gossip about others. But on some level, you're being judged (negatively) when you pass such information along. Save your hot secrets for your attorney, your minister, priest, rabbi, spouse, or close friend.

In the last chapter, I talked about "associating for success." It's vital. But sometimes our desire to align with someone else can take us into dangerous territory. It can spawn a temptation to speak negatively about someone who you know isn't friendly with the person you want to become closer to.

Believe me, gossiping about someone else is not the way to get there.

At the conferences, seminars, and business meetings I attend, many employers tell me that their businesses are suffering from low employee morale. It's a huge drain on productivity. One potential reason for that low productivity? Employees are spending too much of their time spreading gossip about one another instead of concentrating on their jobs.

There is never justification to gossip about others at work. And that extends to speculating about your company's future.

If you work inside an organization that is under constant change, it's quite natural to experience concern over your security. But resist the temptation to commiserate with customers or with other employees about it.

Instead, make your concern work for you.

A travel agent I know (and have done some business with) told me over the phone the other day that the large agency she has been with for more than fifteen years is a "scary place to work these days." It was obvious from our conversation that she was consumed with worry. I asked her if she had any plans to improve her position inside the organization or to look for another position if conditions continued to worsen. She admitted she hadn't.

I suggested that one plan she could put in place immediately was to commit to being more versatile inside her agency. "Dedicated sales"—that is, being responsible solely for selling a product or service within an organization—is a thing of the past. Many salespeople now take shifts answering phone calls once handled by receptionists. "It's turned out to be an opportunity for me," one real-estate agent told me. "During my phone shift, I've been able to pick up sales leads I wouldn't have otherwise."

The other day I saw one of my top salespersons straightening up a storage closet. She'd chosen to take mental ownership of her workplace, where she spends most of her time. And her act produced a direct benefit. She discovered unpacked brochures and other useful tools that helped her make sales.

The point is that change, no matter how scary, always presents opportunities.

In addition to having a positive attitude about change, I chose to confront change rather than deny it or just "hope for the best." One thing that's been very effective for me (and can work for you, too) is to ask those in management for a briefing as to what's going on and what's ahead. Then I follow up with some kind of statement about how I'm eager to help out. In this way, I'm not asking for assurance from them but rather giving it to them. (I can promise you that people responsible for making changes get scared, too, and usually appreciate offers of help.)

When I was a fairly new car dealer, Chrysler was undergoing a major corporate change. Rumor had it that we were going to lose our local corporate office. Instead, a branch in another city that didn't understand the special needs of our community would be servicing us.

Initially, I, along with other car dealers, felt insecure about all the "what ifs." So I decided to ask questions. And as I got answers, I started seeing things through Chrysler's perspective. Chrysler felt that by consolidating their local offices, they would have more resources in one place that its dealers could draw on. When I offered my help, I was asked to serve on a council of car dealers to meet with Chrysler regularly to share input. Our helplessness converted to helpfulness. We did lose our branch office, with all of the familiar faces and relationships we'd developed over the years. But before long, I was meeting new people and getting fresh ideas, which benefited my business.

You're more likely to be part of the team creating solutions if you express a willingness to ride the wave of change. It sure beats just gossiping or worrying about it.

Many of us at some time in our career are asked to tackle more responsibility even in lesser roles. One could look at it as a negative, but that won't get you anywhere. If you look at the situation the other way, you may realize there are fewer employees—fewer fish in the tank—right now. It's an opportunity—an opportunity to get noticed. An opportunity for personal development and growth. You are needed more than ever. Remember that the essence of selling is helping others—and that includes those within your company.

## 9.2    There Is a Time to Sell—and a Time Not to Sell

I'm often asked car questions at social functions where the other people present are not interested in long, elaborate answers. The questions range from "How much longer is Chrysler going to be offering rebates on their minivans?" to "Is it possible for my daughter to buy a car on her own without me cosigning?" to "Has the merger between Chrysler and Daimler [Mercedes] been good for consumers?"

Because I don't want to offend listeners in the periphery who are uninterested, no matter what the question, my response is short, while honoring the person asking the question with a consistent "A,B,C" reply.

A: I tell them tactfully that this is not the place for me to properly answer their question.

B: I touch lightly on why we need a better time and place. (Three sentences or less!)

C: I invite them to join me at another time and place.

Let me give you an example. Say someone has just asked me whether they are better off leasing or buying a car. Here is my response:

A: "Here tonight, I can offer you only an 'it depends' answer to your question." Or I might say, "You're asking me a great question that deserves more than the short answer I can give you now."

B: "Leasing vs. buying a car has to consider the mileage you'll be putting on it. It also depends on how long you intend to drive the car. And some cars are better candidates for leasing than others, depending upon their residual value—that is, how much they are worth when the lease is up."

C: "Because it takes a while to sort through all the variables, I'd like to offer you my card and an invitation to call me at my office, where we could talk more fully. I'd appreciate the opportunity to be able to discuss this in more detail."

My point is that while there are sales opportunities all around us, there are times when pursuing a sale is the wrong thing to do. There is a thin line between being informative (helpful) and being invasive (hurtful).

There are times when we're given an opportunity to enter into someone else's world because of circumstances beyond our control—to form a relationship with someone we might not have otherwise met. For one thing, it is an opportunity to learn about ourselves, by seeing how we behave and react in sometimes trying conditions. And since relationships always involve a trade of some kind, the way we behave toward and interact with others can help us anywhere we go.

A friend of mine who is a customer service trainer for a large corporation had to go into the hospital for an operation. She is one of the most dynamic women I've ever known, and I couldn't imagine how this ultra-active woman was going to be able to handle what promised to be a lengthy postoperative recuperation, complete with physical therapy.

When I came to visit, there she was propped up in the bed, asking one of the nurses for help in rearranging the many floral arrangements she had received. "I would be so grateful if you would remove the wilted ones and regroup the healthy ones," she told her. The nurse, obviously acting outside of her job responsibilities, nonetheless uncomplainingly transformed herself into a florist, giving the room a beautifying treatment.

"Anything for you, honey. You make my job so pleasant," she responded.

After the nurse finished, I commented to my friend on the treatment she'd received. "Well, the nurse is a sweet lady," she said. "And she has some beautiful grandchildren."

It became obvious to me that my friend had taken an interest in the nurse's life. And in doing so, she'd unintentionally improved her own, as well, even under trying circumstances. Because she had shown an interest in the nurse's life, and had nourished that newfound relationship before making her appeal, her own requests received equally special treatment.

Persuasion is an art, because it has many variations. But it always starts with taking a genuine interest in the other person.

## 9.3 Say Thank You

Expressing appreciation works wonders. It is probably the most underestimated gesture in any relationship. Our mothers knew how vital it was. Chances are those two words, "thank you," were among the first you were taught to say. Mothers everywhere are heard daily reminding their toddlers to "tell the lady thank you." Yet, somewhere between adolescence and early adulthood, many people minimize or forget the importance of expressing appreciation.

We're all more apt to do things for others—our friends, relatives, coworkers, or employers—who express appreciation to us. It's that basic. (How many divorced couples cite "lack of appreciation" as the beginning of their downfall?) I will even go so far as to say that without expressing appreciation, your most artful attempts at persuasion won't work.

When a customer tells a customer service agent with the city's water department, "I would really appreciate your help in verifying the accuracy of my water bill. It was extraordinarily high," he is much more likely to get an answer than is a customer who calls with a sense of entitlement or anger.

People simply don't run on empty. They've got to be fed, nourished—and that includes emotional nourishment. Too often we get a bit stale (notice the "we") in using our good manners, even with the people we know best and care about the most.

## 9.4    Prospecting Outside of the Box

I was with my preteen niece, Lauren, at a local shopping mall the other day, when a beautiful twenty-something girl approached us. "Your daughter is so beautiful. I'd like to invite her to our modeling call next week," she said. At the woman's words, Lauren broke into a smile—one I'd never seen before. Her excitement was almost uncontainable.

After I made the correction about our relationship, I explained that Lauren was just visiting me and lived in another city. The young woman said that was fine; she was recruiting for the entire state and had "calls" scheduled in many locations.

I took the information and her business card. Before we were out of the store, Lauren was already reaching for my cell phone to call her mom.

As we continued our shopping, I couldn't help but think how effective this sales outreach must be. What better place to find young, female modeling recruits than at a mall!

And that is a perfect example of what to do to turn the "box" inside out.

There is pressure on us all to come up with new ways to let people know what we have to offer. Having a nice ad in the phone book or the newspaper is no longer enough. We've got to look for ways to help prospective customers think of coming to us.

At some level, I've always known this. I remember, as a car salesperson, standing at the gate of a nearby pants factory at quitting time to pass out car brochures with my business card stapled to them to workers walking out to their cars. My cards had a special sales inducement—I offered them a hundred free gallons of gas with the purchase of a new car. (I had arranged with the dealership for the cost of the gas to be deducted from my commissions. Management applauded my "ingenuity and ambition" and gladly facilitated the accounting.)

I repeated the same approach at hair salons, teachers' lounges, nurses' stations, anywhere there was a congregation of women.

Clearly, I was drawing on one of my primary assets—the fact that I am a woman. Where appropriate, I would tell the women I met that I was a single mom, a car "salesman" who catered to women. Many times a woman would pull me off to the side to consult with me about her situation. She might tell me she needed a car but had no down payment. Or confess to having no credit or bad credit. Many times I was able to help her solve her problem.

I made certain, however, that I never interrupted anyone while she was working—a seamstress at her sewing machine, for example, or a stylist cutting hair. (There were times I had to simply leave my "samples" at the front desk.)

My idea—crude as it was—worked. It was exciting to hear the results of my efforts—"Marion, you have a customer in the showroom"—come across the paging system. It was even more exciting to walk to the reception area and respond to the customer standing there holding my brochure and business card.

Looking back, I don't think there's ever been a time when I depended solely on traditional ways of prospecting. Perhaps I was relying on my female intuition. I accepted that people in general—and especially women—rate the experience of buying a car about even with going through a tax audit. I felt that if they got a chance to meet a "different kind of car salesman" (and on their own turf), they might be more at ease visiting a car dealership. I knew there were only so many sales phone inquiries (in the car business they're called "phone-ups") to go around. I considered it part of my responsibility to my employer to create my own "following"—customers who would call in to ask for *me*. I've always looked for ways to give them a reason.

Selling outside of the store is something I've always encouraged my employees, seminar students, and conference attendees to do, as well. If you're selling a cosmetic line, offer samples at a women's luncheon. If you list homes, offer a certificate for a complimentary home-listing sales-assessment consultation. Throw in a free houseplant. If you are an interior decorator, offer a sample of your work to a furniture store in exchange for referrals.

When a fledgling and, in my opinion, very talented artist was a bit frustrated that she hadn't been able to sell much of her work, I suggested that she donate some of her pieces to charitable organizations to assist them with their fund-raising efforts. By doing so, she would also get her work seen at community functions.

The first silent auction of one of her favorite pieces brought in $500. She continued to donate, and within the first year she was credited with raising thousands of dollars for good causes.

Sometime later, she told me that she was in the midst of preparing for a job-performance review to be conducted by a twelve-member board she answered to. (Her "day job" is in banking.) With some help from me, her updated, one-page bio included the words *"an accomplished artist whose paintings have raised large sums of money for numerous national charities."* She left the meeting with not only a raise but with two appointments to show her artwork!

Every employer, whether he or she is a manager, supervisor, board director, or customer, wants to feel that they've selected a terrific person to do the job. Use your assets to create new ways for people to learn about what you do. It's a sure way to widen your circle of influence.

---

- **You are always on stage.** People are constantly making judgments about you in and outside the workplace. Use that fact to your advantage.

- **Parties and other outside functions are good places to meet people (including potential customers).** But put up strict boundaries on sales presentations. No one likes a pushy salesperson, and they like one less outside of the store.

- **Create opportunities to sell outside the box.** Even if you have the better mousetrap, it can take a long time for the world to beat a path to your door. Instead of waiting for customers to come to you, look for nontraditional ways to attract them and go where they are.

---

# Chapter 10

# HOW TO COUNTER "I'M JUST LOOKING"

Before I started writing this book, I asked several friends if there were topics that they particularly wanted me to cover. Over and over again I heard (especially from those in traditional sales), "You have to deal with the question of what to do when customers say, 'I'm just looking.'"

At first, it seemed odd that there should be such a universal cry for information about such a small part of the sale. Wasn't it obvious that customers all want time and space to look before they buy? That's *why* they give that universal response, "I'm just looking."

"That's fine and good," one friend told me. "But understanding why customers say it doesn't help me know what I should say or do next."

Finally convinced that I needed to address these three bothersome words, I gave them a great deal of thought. It reminded me how powerful words can be. They can intimidate and discourage (which seemed to be the case when a customer claimed he or she was just looking), even among those who are good at sales. Words may not break bones, but they *can* affect us. And they can be misleading at times—intentionally or not.

Look at the way politicians use words. President Bush referred to *going to war* as a "freedom initiative." The military tells us there were a hundred "casualties," rather than a hundred *people* hurt or killed. In journalism, "misreporting" is a sanitized way of saying that the reporter screwed up, big time. And in car sales, "pre-owned" cars sell much better than *used* ones.

"Spin doctors" have become *the* profession of the new millennium. But the meaning of words can shift, depending on the speaker and the listener. Sometimes we hear more than what is meant.

And sometimes we hear what's not meant at all. That is often the case when a customer says, "I'm just looking." If you listen carefully, "I'm just looking" may be a call for help.

As women, we have an advantage when it comes to active listening. Women are inherently good listeners. Even most men I know would agree that on the whole we're better at picking up on tone, volume, pauses, and general body-language cues when people talk. Often there is a great deal of meaning behind what's *not* being said. And we're sensitive to it.

When a customer says, "I'm just looking," the truth is that he or she is "just looking" *for now*. That customer is not ready to buy *yet*. He or she may need more information, and *for now* this is their way of getting it.

In my early days, when a customer told me they were "just looking," I'd think it meant "I don't like you." Feeling rejected, I was prevented from putting my best foot forward. I would become paralyzed.

And those times when I managed not to feel rejected, I felt discouraged, thinking this was a customer who was not serious about buying a car and was only "killing time." (In the car business, we call them "tire kickers.")

Early on, "I'm just looking" was the most common customer response to my initial offer of help. It wasn't long before I realized that I needed to desensitize myself a bit and start hearing these three words differently. My frustration and rejection were impairing my ability to be professional. Let's face it: It's hard to persuade someone of something from a position of pain.

So, what *should* you do to prevent feeling rejected and discouraged? How can you turn an "I'm just looking" into an "I want to buy . . ."?

## 10.1   The Most Natural Part of the Buying Cycle

First, remember that customers *have* to look before they buy, whether buying in a store or through a mail-order catalogue.

Customers who shop on the Internet "surf," "browse," "download," and compare their options relentlessly. (Indeed, there are entire Web sites, such as MySimon.com, devoted to such browsing.) Large companies, too, look at various proposals before they buy. As individuals, we date before we marry. Looking is a natural part of *every* buying process.

The fact that customers are "just looking" doesn't mean they will never do more. It just means that they are not ready to buy this minute. And it doesn't mean that they don't want to buy from *you*. It means that they are not ready to buy from *anyone* right now.

In the car business, the average time between a customer first stepping foot on a car lot and driving away in a new car is seventy-two hours. Granted, the buying cycle might be a bit longer for purchasers of nuclear power plants (and shorter for buyers of a pair of jeans), but the premise is the same: "I'm just looking" *always* precedes buying!

On the other hand, sometimes customers say, "I'm just looking" as a means of disguising their ignorance. I know I have done that.

I recently went shopping for a new home computer for my husband's birthday. (Though I'm not computer illiterate, I must confess that technological matters have been for the most part something I've been quick to delegate at our dealerships.) There I was at a chain electronics store surrounded by more computers than I can remember. I didn't know where to begin the shopping process. A young man approached me and asked if he could help me. Without even thinking twice about it, I responded, "I'm just looking."

Clearly, I needed some help, but I didn't know what kind of help to ask for. Not wanting to make a fool of myself, I created some space between the two of us. To his credit, the young salesclerk could sense my discomfort; "I've condensed the differences in most of these computers to one sheet of paper," he said, pointing to his desk a few feet away. He understood that sometimes customers need help to look.

The end of the story? My husband had a super birthday—complete with a high-tech computer system I bought from the extremely knowledgeable and helpful salesperson.

Remember, one person's quite genuine "I'm just looking" might be another person's way to save face. If you are a salesperson who's poised to be *helpful*, you won't feel *helpless* when you hear a customer speak those words.

## 10.2   How to Help Customers Look

It may seem like a special challenge to help someone who declines the need for it. But I have found that if I adhere to a couple of basic guidelines, it's not difficult at all.

One of the first things I discovered was that I was offering my help in a way that invited rejection. I would ask, "May I help you?"

Most people (80 to 90 percent) would simply say, "No, thank you. I'm just looking." I know now that such a yes-or-no question almost begs for a negative response.

Later, I changed it to "May I assist you?" Unfortunately, it wasn't much better.

It was only when I began asking, "*How* may I be of assistance?" that I started getting more information from customers—but only slightly. Once in a while, I'd get a response like "Point me in the direction of your convertibles." But at least 70 percent of the time I was still hearing "I'm just looking."

Through experience (more like trial and error), my greeting evolved to include a more effective opener. I came to realize that customers need a reason to seek you out. (Remember the computer salesman I encountered who offered a one-page comparison report?)

Here's what worked for me. I would walk toward my customers *after* they had gotten out of their car, and with a smile (!) say, "Hi, I'm Marion. Welcome to Love Chrysler. There's a *lot*—no pun intended—to look at here. I carry a key (as I held up my lockbox key) that can open up any vehicle on the lot." In my short greeting, I was able to introduce myself, welcome them, offer a small serving of humor (always a good bond), and most important of all, the KEY (yes, pun intended) reason for my being there—to help them.

Even for those customers who still expressed a desire to look on their own—now down to less than half—I still managed to let them know that I was in a position to help them look better. Before walking away, I would say, "I'll be close by should you wish to take a look at the interior of any particular car." Then I made certain that I positioned myself within their view.

I honored their space. I yielded to their desire. Yet I made sure that I presented myself as someone who could help them "look" better whenever they decided they were ready to.

A wine distributor I know typically visits with customers in the various liquor stores she calls on. One day she noticed a lady combing an aisle stocked with red wines. The woman would pick up various bottles of wine and study their labels and then put them down. When approached by the distributor, she commented that she was—you got it—"just looking."

"I have this catalog here which pairs my wines with various foods," the wine expert mentioned. "Though I make my living selling wines, I have to refer to it often."

After a bit more looking, the customer turned to the distributor (standing only a few feet away) and said, "Maybe you *can* help me. I've been placed in charge of the wine for an upcoming dinner function, and I'm not a wine drinker."

The wine salesperson did three things perfectly, the way I see it. One: She offered a resource (a reason for the customer to seek her out). Two: She offered her help in a way that didn't make the customer feel ignorant. (She invited sharing by sharing her vulnerable side.) Three: She honored the customer's indirect request for space, but yet she didn't disappear from the planet. Put another way: Remain accessible.

In this instance, the distributor/salesperson recognized that the customer probably needed some assistance but didn't know how to ask for it. It's hard for a customer to ask for help when they have no idea what it is they're looking for. That's why it's important that *you* not come off as some kind of know-it-all. That will just distance you from your customer. I recommend the contrary: When appropriate, share a confidence about your vulnerability (as the wine distributor did by admitting even she has to refer to her catalog often). It creates closeness between you and your customer.

When it comes to selling items like jewelry, sunglasses, or purses that are housed inside a showcase or otherwise out of the customer's reach, you have a golden opportunity to become helpful. Allow the customer to touch the merchandise.

It may seem like this should be obvious to salespeople, but it's not. One time I was shopping for a designer handbag for my mother in an extremely upscale store. (It was my mother's birthday.) I wasn't sure what I wanted and I wasn't familiar with their prices. I needed help—but it was like pulling teeth to get it. I tried to take a closer look at a particular purse displayed on a shelf behind the case. And eventually a saleswoman came over and showed it to me. Then, after looking closely at another purse, I asked to see the first one again so that I could compare styles. "You've already looked at that one," the saleslady replied. As I walked out past the security guard, I couldn't help but think they didn't need a security guard—with salespeople like that, it was hard enough to *buy* anything there, let alone steal it! (FYI: I ended up buying my mother a designer handbag at a different store, one that was much more accommodating.)

Customers need to be able to look and compare. It's a natural part of the buying process. Instead of fighting that, why not create venues that give customers a reason to come and look?

As I discussed earlier, I host "How to Buy a Car" clinics on a regular basis. And though I don't offer anything for sale on those nights, I also don't cover my cars with a tarp. They are all on display if the customer wants to look. I drive a "demonstrator" everywhere I go. I purposely leave it parked in a high-traffic area of the parking lot at the airport when I'm traveling. I also provide the president of our local university a demonstrator to drive. After all, he attends every high-profile event in the community. (And I get the satisfaction that comes from donating something for the betterment of education.)

I park cars inside the busiest malls during the long weekend following Thanksgiving. Though the rent is high, so is the exposure to our new models. My salespersons practically fight to be assigned "mall duty," because they know the positive results from customers getting to "look." During any one of those long weekends, we'll see a 50 percent increase in sales.

There's a saying in the car business: "If it's not rolled, it won't be sold." In other words, customers don't buy cars they don't test-drive first. In the car industry, that's part of the looking process. And it is a pretty common phenomenon. I don't know about you, but I'm not inclined to buy a dress I don't first try on. I have to look at it on *me*. Perfume retailers invite you to sample their perfumes on your skin. Builders and real-estate companies host open houses. Department stores know that window-shopping leads to buying. Attorneys host estate-planning conferences.

Bridal fairs, car shows, and trade shows are all planned for the purpose of whetting the appetites of prospective customers.

The next time you hear a customer say, "I'm just looking," think about the story I once heard a sales manager repeat at a sales meeting: "I was 'just looking' when I found my wife!"

---

■ **When you hear a customer say "just looking" . . .** you need to hear the two words they are *not* saying—"I'm just looking *for now*." Don't take it as rejection. Find a way to help your customer look better. If you do, you'll likely make the sale.

■ **To engage the customer,** give them a reason to need you. Come up with some information you can share with them.

■ **Be available.** After the customer says, "I'm just looking," and you give them a reason to eventually seek you out, don't disappear. You don't need to hover near them. But you should remain in their line of sight so that they are able to call for you. The odds are they will!

---

# Chapter 11

# YOU DON'T HAVE TO LIKE THEM—BUT *THEY* HAVE TO LIKE *YOU*

N o one who deals with the public (and that's all of us) can afford not to be liked.

There might have been a time when—if your offering was extremely specialized—you might have been exempt from this rule. But not any longer. Even the best surgeons are learning the worth of "bedside manner." In fact, patient-sensitivity training is now a standard part of the curriculum at most medical schools. Studies have shown that healing environments influence a patient's recovery. And how good can a healing environment be when it is undermined by a negative doctor-patient relationship?

In today's world—where if you're living, you're selling—no amount of credentials can circumvent the need to have people like you. It doesn't matter how many letters you have after your name. If you're disliked in your chosen profession, you're not going to get far. No matter how talented you are, there is always someone else just about as good. And if people like them more, you are going to lose out. That is true if you are a surgeon, a salesman, or anyone else.

As I said before, every transaction requires a relationship, and simply put, *your relationships will run more smoothly if the other person likes you.*

"I don't need you to like me. I just need you to respect me," I once heard a sales manager say. To me, that statement in and of itself made him somewhat unlikable. By making it, he projected an aura of not caring. The truth is, it's in our nature as human beings to want to bond with other people. And none of us wants to align ourselves with a person who professes from the beginning not to need our esteem.

Another truth: It's hard to respect someone you don't like. I can't even think of an example to offer you of a person I've respected but didn't like. My sales manager fell far short of earning his staff's respect. And he sure wasn't liked. (Not surprisingly, his tenure was short-lived.)

Do you need to like the other party in the relationship? True to the title of this chapter, you don't *have* to like them. (Of course, if you're selling to someone you *do* like, it makes the experience more pleasant.)

In sales, you deal with all kinds, as the cliché goes.

At times in my career, I have seen the greediest sides of people. People can be hard to handle. I have dedicated an entire later chapter to dealing with difficult people. So let's move on to the business of getting people to like *you.*

## 11.1    Never Sell Yourself Short

There are many things you can do to make yourself more lik-able. In the pages that follow, I emphasize six (somewhat coun-terintuitive) principles that have worked for me. I know they can work for you. But first I want to offer a couple of important disclaimers.

I do *not* advocate trying to be liked at all costs. Selling your-self short, compromising your integrity or individuality in the name of being liked, is never worthwhile. If you present your-self as someone you're not and people like you, they like some-one you're not. And what will follow from that is you'll end up not liking yourself.

When your need to be liked by other people dictates your life, your self-esteem is the casualty. I would never suggest that you live a life guided by the opinions of others. I would never advocate anything that would cause you to relinquish your sense of self or personal power. In fact, if other people know that you're living a life dictated by your need to be liked—and they realize you are willing to compromise your beliefs to make that happen—it sabotages your position in any transaction. Whether you're negotiating a raise, asking for a date, or negoti-ating the sale of your home, if you're obsessive about being liked, you're operating from a position of weakness.

It is not my intention to say or write anything that would cause you to put your own convictions and self-respect aside.

Having said that, to be successful in life, we need help from others. And people are a lot more apt to want to help us if they like us.

## 11.2     Six Tried-and-Tested Ways to Be More Likable

In the world of traditional sales, you're selling three things: product, price, and self. And I feel that of the three things you're selling, self has the most impact. When people like you, they are more likely to forgive your (slight) lack of product knowledge, or even your (slightly) higher price. I used the word "slight" because there are limits, of course. No amount of charm can overcome complete product ignorance or unfair price gouging. But if people like you, they *want* to see you succeed. As a result, they will go out of their way to buy from you. There is probably no greater satisfaction in sales than when a customer expresses not only appreciation for your help but also a liking for *you*. I recall one such incident when a woman bought her very first Chrysler from me. "I can't say I like this car better than the Toyotas I've always owned," she said. "But I know I feel good about buying from you."

Let's take a look at some of the stratagems you might not have given much thought to.

**1. Create ways for people to identify you with *their* positive emotions.**

It's human nature for us to dislike someone we associate with a negative experience. "I trust my gynecologist, but I don't *like* him," a friend recently told me. After I probed a bit, I learned that she's never undergone anything but routine exams from this doctor. (And most of you reading can identify with how *un*fun those are.) He's never been in a position to save her life or offer her relief (a positive emotion) from any kind of pain. But the same woman loves her dentist. "He's great," she said. It seems that during her last visit to him he was able to offer her immediate and permanent relief from a severe toothache. While the actual experience (a root canal) was probably less than pleasurable, he rescued her, so to speak. Or, put another way, he restored her to a feeling of well-being.

But you don't have to be in the business of rescuing people to be likable. *Take a good look at what makes someone feel good and identify yourself with it in some way.* It's something any of us can do.

When it was time to name my first car dealership, I considered many possibilities. My name on a sign didn't much turn me on, so I thought up many alternatives. The name "love" was by far the most appealing to me, and I felt confident it would be to others, as well. After all, it's probably the most positive word in our vocabulary. It stirs up good feelings in all of us. By choosing the name "love," I was in a sense associating my operation with a positive emotion that everyone could identify with. And so we became Love Chrysler.

When it was time to name my second dealership, I didn't have to think twice. By then I could say that I was "spreading 'Love' all over Texas!" Our second store name is Love Chrysler Dodge Jeep. To further connect my businesses to the emotion of love, I chose Valentine's Day as the holiday my car dealerships are identified with. Each year we host a "couples sale." My advertisements go something like this:

*Valentine's Day is a time when couples celebrate their love. At Love Chrysler, we're celebrating couples. Buy one; get a couple. When you purchase any new car from Love this Valentine's Day, you receive a pre-owned car from this selection, FREE! Buy one; get a couple. But you better hurry. This offer is good only one day (not a couple), and only at Love.*

During one part of the spot, the camera pans the "selection" of cars offered as the free ones. They're truly good cars—well-maintained backup family cars, fishing cars, cars for teenagers.

As you might imagine, the response is tremendous. People ask me all the time how I can afford to do it. "Do you make a profit on that day?" they ask. Directly? No. But it's hard to measure the long-term, overall benefit to my businesses that's realized as a result of not so much giving cars away, but rather of creating a *wow!* association with a day that celebrates our namesake—a namesake that evokes warm feelings in everyone.

You don't have to give anything away to imply a connection between you and positive emotions held by someone. You can simply *be a bearer of good tidings whenever possible.* (It's the opposite of the idea "shoot the messenger.") For example, the gynecologist I mentioned earlier would probably be more likable to his patients if he delivered the "normal" test results himself. (Instead, he has his nurse call, followed by a cold form letter.)

For example: "Ms. Jones, this is Dr. So-and-so. I wanted to call you personally to share the good news of your test results. All indications are that you are in good health."

And notice the *feeling* words used by the doctor in this example: "You are in good health" as compared to "Your test results were normal" (spoken by the nurse).

A good addendum to the "be the bearer of good tidings" idea is to *make good use of words that generate a sense of personal connection.* In the car-selling business, typically a salesman might say, "Notice this one-touch, keyless door-entry system." I would advise, "Notice this *convenient*, one-touch, keyless door-entry system designed with your *security* and *safety* in mind." If you're selling cosmetics, what sounds more inviting—"This foundation will give your complexion a glow" or "This foundation will give your complexion a *healthy* glow"? And if you're selling real estate, what sounds more touching—"Homes in this neighborhood have good resale value" or "Owning a home in this neighborhood *protects* your investment"? Convenience, security, safety, health, protection. They're all words that conjure up good feelings in all of us.

I'm not suggesting that you gush adjectives at every turn. But I am saying that making an attempt to touch people's emotions in a way that connects them to what you are selling is good. As women, we have long been accused of being "emotional." That, I firmly believe, is a good thing in sales. After all, purchases are emotional experiences.

## 2. Let your human side show.

Let me confess: I am a recovering perfectionist.

There was a time when I would host a family Thanksgiving dinner and be so absorbed with every detail—the turkey had to look like it was ready for a magazine cover; the pies had to be made "from scratch"; the linen napkins had to be ironed just so—that the true meaning of the holiday escaped me entirely.

In fact, any event I hosted in my home had to be perfect—perfectly planned and perfectly executed. Then came a defining moment when I learned that *perfectionism is not a likable trait*.

One evening when I was attending a dinner party at a friend's home, the hostess told me, "I hope you think everything's okay. I've been nervous all week about you coming. Your affairs are always so perfect."

Boom! It hit me. How perfect were my affairs if they made people I cared about feel intimidated or inadequate? (Little did she know how much stress I went through before and during each affair.) I decided that night to take a second look at this trait of mine.

I looked at the ways my perfectionism affected my business and my life. It became clear to me, once I wiped off the lens I was looking through, that I had put off many projects because I wasn't in a position to carry them off perfectly. I couldn't finish creating the promotional mailers I had in my head until I completely cleaned off my desk so that I could "concentrate" on them. I couldn't straighten up my jewelry box until I could overhaul the closet it was in. Procrastination had, in many instances, replaced progress, and that led to stress. And stress, I learned, is contagious. My employees were showing signs of stress: absences, costly mistakes, low productivity, and, worst of all, turnover.

I had been a perfectionist to impress people. (It is a sign of insecurity—although I didn't see it that way at the time.) I had impressed them, all right. They were impressed enough with me to have to think twice about inviting me into their homes. They were impressed enough with me to want to go work for someone else. ("I'm just not perfect," one assistant told me during her exit interview. I hadn't wanted her to leave, but she felt she had to because there was no way to live up to my standards.) My efforts had been counterproductive.

Once I became aware of this, I was able to start making some changes. But it took courage to change the way I had always done things.

I started out small. I gave myself permission to relax, take shortcuts, and be frivolous. For hors d'oeuvres for a card game, I made finger foods that everyone liked but that didn't "go together"—chicken salad sandwiches served alongside bean-

and-cheese burritos. Before, I wouldn't have scheduled the get-together until I had found the time to plan and prepare a "theme"—South of the Border or Polynesian cuisine. And, of course, I would have had to coordinate the food with the right party favors and libations.

At work, I'd tidy up a file as opposed to overhauling the entire system. I'd hold spontaneous mini-meetings as opposed to meetings scheduled long in advance with well-planned agendas.

It wasn't long before I started noticing positive differences in my relationships with people—personally and professionally. People seemed to want to be around me more. And it wasn't long before I realized that people liked me, flaws and all.

Of course, I'm not advocating that you loosen your standards to the point that you become sloppy or scatterbrained. What I am saying is that *the poorest excuse for doing nothing is that you can't do it perfectly.*

### 3. Accentuate similarities.

I talked about this earlier: People like doing business with people they see as similar to themselves. Well, I want to take that concept one step further. People like people who are (almost) exactly like them. And if someone likes you, you're a lot more apt to earn their trust—an essential building block in any relationship.

I was once a character witness in a civil trial. I won't go into all of the details out of respect for the people involved, but during a break after offering my testimony, I was applauded by the attorneys who had called me to the stand, for the way I had "endeared" myself with the jury. It seems that in the course of my testimony, I had revealed that I had been a teenage parent. Because I had made that one statement, several members of the jury (who had—as I learned later—also been teen parents) were able to "identify" with me and therefore liked me better. And because I was liked, I was trusted and more credible!

In the same light, my experience as a breast cancer survivor (I prefer to say "thriver") is one that has enrolled me into a sisterhood of women. Wherever, whenever I speak to an audience, inevitably women come up to me after my speech to tell me how they, too, went through a similar experience. It's almost as if we've known each other forever. I suppose that's why war veterans are so close. High school reunions have endured for generations because of this principle. *Bonding is created by a shared experience.*

But how do you go about finding commonalities between yourself and a complete stranger? Women may be able to draw from their inherent curiosity about other people (men sometimes call it being nosy).

My husband, Tim, is constantly amazed at how quickly I'm able to get to know people. I tend to ask questions about the other person, such as "Do you have any children?" or "Is this your first visit to Hawaii?"—depending on the time, the place, or the purpose. If you show an interest in someone, they're bound to reveal things about themselves.

Once you have that information, you can work toward building a relationship based on similarities.

### 4. Be a good receiver.

As girls, we were all taught to be "nice." But sometimes it helps to let other people do nice things for you.

The act of giving makes people feel good. If you're good at receiving, you're effectively *inviting* the person who is giving to feel good about themselves. And *how people feel about themselves is bound to reflect on how they feel about you.*

Let's take compliments. We all know how good we feel when we receive one. In fact, we sometimes feel so good that we want to hear it repeated.

"I love your new hairstyle," someone says.

"Do you really like it?" we ask.

But a better way to receive a compliment—one that allows the person to feel good about giving it—might be to respond, "Thank you. You just made my day." That kind of appreciation is bound to make the person who gave the compliment feel important, generous, just plain good! And by extension, when they feel good about their own act, they'll find you more likable.

Our well-meaning teachers in life told us that it is by giving that people come to like us. And if you're like me, you learned that lesson well (and have been giving all of your life). But somewhere along the way we ignored the importance of receiving. Oh sure, we learned how to send thank-you cards and respond with all of the polite niceties. But we probably stopped there, not realizing that by not being properly responsive when we have been on the receiving end, we have probably cost ourselves the opportunity to make more friends.

Let me give you an example. I called a friend the other day whom I hadn't seen in a while to ask her to lunch to "catch up." She accepted my invitation, but with some reservation in her voice. We had a perfectly nice lunch, and finally, when the check came, I automatically reached for it. She stopped me, confessing, "In case you hadn't noticed, I've stopped initiating any get-togethers with you for this very reason. You always pay. It makes me feel bad."

At first, I couldn't believe it. I felt that my generosity had been attacked.

In the end, she won the tug-of-war over the check and we left.

Upon reflection later, I realized how wrong I had been.

I had thought that because my income was greater than hers it should be assumed that I would do the paying. What I hadn't realized was that she had felt, in effect, shortchanged—not able to give fully to the relationship. In her eyes (temporarily only, thank goodness), I had become less likable.

We now alternate who pays. And *I* have learned the value of receiving.

### 5. Like them first.

Back in the days when I was a saleswoman, my boss learned that I was being recruited by another dealership. He called me into his office and addressed the issue head-on. "Your earning potential is unlimited here," he said. "But there's another thing I want you to consider even more. I'm speaking for the entire management team when I say that not only do we like the job you do, we like you." (I ended up staying on—that is, until I moved on to a management job at another dealership about a year later.) That example speaks to an important principle. *It's very tough for someone not to like you if you like them first.* That's why it's so important that when you like someone, you not keep it a secret. Tell them.

### 6. Laugh.

Whenever I pass by a salesperson's office and I hear them exchanging laughter with a customer, I know that a sale is in progress. Laughing together is the best relationship glue I know of.

Humor is perhaps the best way to break the ice of an awkward introduction, to relax a stressful situation, and to put yourself in a likable light. But what if you're not the stand-up-comedienne type? That doesn't prevent you from laughing at another person's jokes, quips, or wit. If you can't initiate it, at least learn to follow along.

I know a saleslady who enjoys great success in the field of fundraising for a national charity. It might seem odd to you, given her profession, that she describes herself as the "shy type." And I think she's probably pretty accurate in her self-description— she's somewhat on the quiet side. That is, except for her laugh. Her laugh, while feminine, is hearty and contagious. People want to be around her because her good spirits just permeate the room. She has found success in her chosen field in spite of her shyness, because she has the "gift of laughter."

■ **You aren't going to like all of your customers.** Human beings are just too diverse to like them all. But it is important that they like you. If people don't like you, it is sooooooooooo much harder to make a sale.

■ **Give them reasons to like you.** Put yourself in situations where customers will associate you with pleasant experiences.

■ **But never lose your sense of who you *really* are.** If you do, you'll lose your self-respect and the respect of your customer. No one likes a phony.

# Chapter 12

# TAKING CHARGE OF THE SALES PROCESS

I can't count the times the all-male management team I sold cars under told me that "control" was the name of the game. "If you can't control the customer, you can forget about making the sale," they told me over and over again. I even heard advice on how to "seize control" from the very moment you meet a potential customer. "Ask questions early on that will get a customer to say yes," they'd tell me. (Are you enjoying the good weather we've been having?) "If you do that, you'll be more likely to get a customer to say yes later to the big question." (Are you ready to buy?)

Well, I didn't feel comfortable with the role they wanted me to play. I thought that if I followed their advice I would be tricking people. So I had to create another way to spur sales. After all, even if I were able to succeed in sales using the control-the-customer business model, I didn't *want* to be perceived as a controlling woman. (Let's face it. Men can wear the "controller" label in our society a lot more easily than women.) The stereo-type of a controlling businesswoman is one who abuses her employees by working them long hours for unfair (and some-times illegal) wages, neglects her children, browbeats her hus-band, and turns her back on her aging, ailing parents. That picture was certainly not compatible with the person I wanted to become.

Maybe I've watched too many Joan Crawford movies (I love classics) like *Mildred Pierce*, *Queen Bee*, and *Harriet Craig*. In each one, Crawford portrayed a woman who lied to, cheated, and used people, all in the name of pursuing her goals. In the end, she always became the victim of her own unhealthy ambi-tion. I didn't want that to happen to me.

And so I decided I would seize control of no one other than myself. And with that decision, I set out to take charge of my career.

Intuitively, I've always known that customers don't want to—nor should they ever have to—relinquish control of decid-ing what's best for them. But to make wise decisions, customers *do* need the benefit of expert information. And it's a salesper-son's responsibility to see that they get it by taking charge of the sales process.

It's important to understand the difference between taking charge and taking control.

I think it's safe to assume that we've all purchased something at one time or another from an overbearing, controlling sales-person. Here are a few examples of such a person:

- The salesperson who uses tactics such as insults, embarrass-ment, and being judgmental to push people into compliance. I'm reminded here of the real-estate agent who told a client who was worried about her ability to make the mortgage payments, "You've been throwing your money away on rent for years. It'd be ignorant of you not to sign the papers that are going to make you a homeowner."

- The salesperson who uses threats to get her way. And yes, that includes little ones like "It will more than likely be sold by the time you make up your mind." I remember hearing a salesman, as he watched a couple turn into the driveway, say, "Oh, good. They're back. The car they've been thinking about is already sold. I tried to warn them. I'm going to enjoy telling them." I couldn't believe it actually turned him on to be able to say, "I told you so." Talk about confused priorities.

- The salesperson who gloats about his position. "I'm the only one in town who can sell you this top name brand. Here are my terms." My-way-or-the-highway presentations are abrasive, and when they do work they leave a customer feeling more like a hostage than a privileged client.

The biggest problem with bullying a customer into making a decision that's not right for them is that you forfeit the potential for them to become a repeat customer and a source of referrals. If you strong-arm them once (even if it might initially appear that you're successful), don't look for them to return. They will do everything in their power to avoid coming back.

In contrast to controlling the sales process, *taking charge* of the sales process allows you to work *with* your customer. You're acting in your customers' best interest, giving them the best possible information to make the most appropriate buying decision. In other words, you're acting as a virtual "guide." And when customers feel you have acted in their best interest in guiding them down a path of purchasing wisdom, they'll trust you *and* reward you. Plus, they will give you the opportunity to do even more for them (and their friends and relatives) in the future.

I would have been dead in the water a long time ago without my customers acting as my ambassadors. The comment "My neighbor referred me to your dealership here, Ms. Brem" is so nice to hear. And "This makes the fourth car my family has bought here" is music to my ears. Word of mouth is my favorite kind of advertising. I wouldn't sacrifice it for all the control in the world.

## 12.1    Help Your Customers Navigate the Sales Rapids

I recently kayaked down a river in Alaska. The landscape was absolutely gorgeous. But my greatest pleasure came from having a river guide offer an environmentalist's narration of what I was seeing, and preparing me for what lay ahead. I got to learn about the history and biology of the land in a way that enhanced my experience beyond words.

The same thing happens when I go to a museum. I get so much more out of my visit when I listen to the self-guided tour (where narration on what you are seeing is provided via a tape recorder and earphones the museum makes available to rent). I find that artifacts of all kinds take on greater meaning when their historical and/or artistic value is explained.

Having a guide for the *sales* process is every bit as important. After all, the road toward a sale is a scary one for many consumers. For one thing, acquiring something new represents a change in their lives, and most of us are, at least to some degree, resistant to change. For another, you can assume that the process of buying your product—whether it's a car or a casket—is relatively unfamiliar to your customer. Fear of the unknown is almost always stifling. And the cost involved can be considerable, depending on what the customer is buying.

To dispel your customer's fears, it's your responsibility as a salesperson to share your expertise with them in a way that sheds light on the process of buying *and* speaks to them, touching their hot buttons and passions. (More on that in the next chapter.) The information you share will be best received when it's served in small doses, or, as I call it, "step selling." It's the art of taking a customer one step at a time toward the ultimate "asking for the sale." For purposes of illustration, let me go back to my native land of car sales.

## 12.2 Step Selling

My ultimate objective is to have a customer say, "Write it up." But that's not a car salesperson's first goal. For example, if a customer initially makes an Internet or phone inquiry about a particular model, the salesman begins by setting up an in-person appointment with the customer. It might entail taking the vehicle to their home or office, but at some point a face-to-face visit is necessary. So step one in the sales process is meeting the customer.

Once the appointment has been set, or an in-person meeting with the customer who walked in has occurred, a car salesperson's next objective is to have the customer agree to the "test drive." When the customer shows enough interest to get behind the wheel, that goal has been realized. Once the customer feels he has selected the right vehicle, the next step is for the salesperson to invite the customer into her office, where trade-in values, rebates, and financing terms are determined.

And finally, after the customer has made it known that he is comfortable with both the vehicle and the terms, it's up to the salesperson to ask for the sale. This part scares so many salespeople. Mostly, I believe, it's a fear of rejection. (More about that later.) But truly, if every other step has been followed—with the customer's best interests in mind—asking for the sale will not only be expected by the customer, it will be welcomed.

## 12.3　Don't Speak in Slang

In every sale, each step of the way, a salesperson is responsible for explaining what comes next—and in a language the customer can understand. Be careful not to use acronyms and industry slang. Too often I've heard car salesmen make statements to a customer that provoked more confusion than enlightenment. "I'm going to get the ACV on your trade," said one. Translation? "I'm going to take the car you're currently driving to the manager who specializes in appraising pre-owned vehicles. I'll be returning with a figure that will represent what its actual cash value [ACV] is. Then we can proceed to calculate what your new monthly payment will be."

I recently reminded a salesman at one of my dealerships that the "Chrysler T & C" I overheard him talking about to a customer over the phone is a "Chrysler Town & Country minivan." It's amazing to me to see just how often salesmen take verbal shortcuts. When we do that, we risk leaving our customers in the dust. Customers want, need, and deserve to take the scenic route toward the sale. Getting to hear "I'll take it" always requires assuming responsible leadership of the sales transaction—again, not by taking control of the customer but by taking charge of every step of the process.

And even after a customer has said, "Write it up," the guide service you are providing for your customer should continue. Listen to the difference between these two presentations straight from showrooms where I've done business.

"The F and I manager will see you next. By then your car should be out of make-ready." Translation? "From here, I'll be escorting you to what we call our Finance and Insurance office, where one of my colleagues will present you with all of the final titling documents—the certificate of ownership and the like. I'll come to show you out when the Finance and Insurance manager pages me signaling me that he's completed his part of the transaction. Then we'll go over the owner's manual and the many features of your new car!"

In another instance, a mortgage loan officer almost lost a sale, or shall I say more correctly, a good customer. My young niece, D'Amber, and her fiancé, Joseph, were in the process of buying their very first home, and needless to say they were very excited. One day I called D'Amber to ask her how the deal was coming. She said, "I don't know, but I don't think good."

It seems that the loan officer had told them that their "debt-to-income ratio" was out of line. Not knowing what that meant, my niece and her fiancé didn't offer any more information (her income from overtime and his from a second job). Until I got involved, they were just sitting in limbo, worrying about whether or not to go to another bank.

Sure, explaining in detail what's happening takes a few more words. But assume your customer wants and needs to hear them—that is, unless they've indicated otherwise.

In essence, what you are doing as you guide your customer through the sales process is schooling them in how your business works. As you go along, be cautious not to patronize them or make them feel ignorant. One way to protect yourself and your customer from that kind of misstep is to preface whatever you're explaining with an invitation for them to interject. This has always worked well for me: "Cut me off if you already know this, but I want to make sure that you have the benefit of all the guidance I'm capable of giving."

## 12.4    Ask Your Customer for a Little Guidance

And while you're in charge of guiding the customer through the sales process, don't be afraid to ask for guidance from them. I've always felt it was important to take the most *appropriate* road toward the sale. For example, it's important to know a customer's price range to avoid wasting their time, as well as possibly getting their hopes set on a vehicle they can't afford. To guide them down the right rows of cars and to help them select the perfect one, I would throw out what I call a "softball question." "In consideration of your time and energy, may I ask what your comfort range is regarding pricing?"

Usually, I hear a helpful response. Maybe they indicate they want to stay under a certain dollar amount. Or they might state that they prefer to keep their payment the same as what it is. These kinds of responses assist me in knowing what direction to take.

But occasionally, I might get a more challenging response, like "Oh, as little as possible." In those cases, I honor their desire to defer price discussions for the time being and ask another soft-ball question, like "Do you have a strong preference in color?" The important thing is that by asking questions, I learn what to do next in the sales process. Inquiring leads to acquiring.

## 12.5   Keep the Menu Simple

Taking charge of the selection process by guiding your customer down the right road should incorporate another consideration. Don't confuse your client with an overabundance of choices. It might seem as if the more options someone has to choose from, the more likely they will be to make a decision. But, in fact, the opposite is true. I have learned that customers actually become more confused and fearful. They start second-guessing what they thought they wanted in the first place.

Here's an example. A male colleague told me he was "very impressed" with a female applicant during an interview. She had experience in human resources. She had experience in public relations. She had experience in marketing as well as technical support. And the list went on. Overwhelmed and uncertain about where he might employ her best, he passed on her altogether! She would have been better off to focus on what *she* wanted and promote herself accordingly.

I'm not suggesting that you should withhold information regarding alternatives a customer should consider. But I am saying that options should be limited to a few select choices. You know you've presented too many when a customer indicates confusion or says that "they're all starting to look alike."

Also, refrain from offering additional choices after the customer has made a selection. Talk about confusion! I was ready to buy a pair of turquoise and silver earrings the other day, when the salesperson at the counter said, "Wait. Let me see what I have under the counter."

I couldn't believe it. I had already said, "They're *exactly* what I've been looking for." I ended up trying on too many and running out of time to pay for any of them! And that brings us to the matter of closing.

## 12.6    A Few Open Words About "Closing"

In sales, no transaction can be consummated without the "close." But in my point of view, which is that of a woman who has enjoyed a reputation as a "closer," we use the wrong term for the act.

Think about it. "Closing" has almost a negative connotation about it. Closing a business means you board the windows. Closing a door means you shut others out. A closed mind is not a pretty thing. I could go on, but the point is that the word "closing" in sales is really a misnomer. When you close a sale, you "open" up a new relationship—one where both parties are better off than before.

I suggest that if salespeople—particularly women, who are more relationship-oriented—changed the way they look at closing a sale, this important step in a sale would be much easier to approach. Since it *is* effectively a beginning, that's an excellent way to ask for the sale. Something along the lines of "May we *begin* the process of ownership now?" or "Shall we *begin* drawing up the paperwork?"

In fact, if you honestly believe that it's in the best interest of a customer to do business with you, you have an obligation to offer them a full opportunity to buy your product and service, and that includes asking them to do so! If you shy away from this process because you fear rejection, you are denying your customer something they have the right to—ownership of your product.

---

■ **Be a guide, not a dictator,** when it comes to the sales process. Show your customer the best way to get where they want to go.

■ **The longest journey starts with but a single step.** Break the sales process into individual steps. Make sure the customer is with you every step of the way.

■ **Stay focused.** Neither you nor your customer should get distracted as you journey toward making the sale.

---

# Chapter 13

# DETERMINING WHAT KIND OF BUYER YOU ARE SELLING TO

## 13.1    What's Passion Got to Do with It?

Taking charge of the sales process is easier when you're on the same wavelength as your customer, speaking *their* language. But it does take a little spadework.

I have discovered over the course of my sales career that "hot buttons" vary among customers, but not as much as you might think. Determining what a customer's hot buttons are makes the sales process go smoother for both parties, the salesperson and the customer, because good communication naturally follows.

By using my experience and interacting with literally thousands of customers and making note of the patterns of details of those relationships, I have come up with a way of categorizing people's *passions* (what motivates them). But before I begin to sound as though I have discovered a miracle cure for cancer, let me say that *passion profiling*—zeroing in on a customer's emotional hot buttons—is as simple as it is helpful. (Obviously, if you can identify what makes somebody want to buy, it's easier to fulfill their needs and close a sale.)

By speaking directly to a customer's passion—their life purpose, their source of personal energy, the things that give meaning and drive to their life—you're more likely to make a connection. And that's what sales are all about.

Women seem to know the importance of emotions instinctively. (Without my love of life and passion for my kids, I never would have been able to put one foot in front of the other during those days on the job when I was suffering the side effects of chemotherapy.) The truth is that the business world across the board is waking up to and recognizing the critical role passion plays as a catalyst for success.

So how can you discover what a person's passion is? How can you determine what motivates them? Easy, as most women know. You ask questions and listen hard to what's said (and what's left unsaid). Let me show you how.

## 13.2   The Four Basic Emotional Makeups of Buyers

I have found that most people typically fall into one of four passion "styles":

**The NOW passion style.** This is the customer who, in the car business, wants the bottom-line price, *now*. Their concern is to get things done expeditiously so that they can move on to the next thing. My strategy in dealing with a NOW passion person? Give them action. Deliver.

Let me give you an example. A well-dressed man in an

expensive suit walked purposefully into our showroom, his eyes scanning the cars intently. When I greeted him, I noticed that his handshake was firm and his voice was confident and strong. "I'm in the market for a company car." Again, his eyes were scanning the showroom.

"Let's get right down to finding you one," I answered.

I proceeded (with a body language that conveyed that I was as decisive as he) to a lineup of stylish sedans. I asked him questions about what he was looking for in terms of color, horsepower, and size, and whether he wanted a four-door or a two-door, as we walked. I had a good idea of what he was looking for by the time we reached the new models.

Before long, he climbed behind the wheel of one and asked, "What's your best price on this one?"

"I suggest you drive it before I price it out for you," I responded. (In the car business, it's a cardinal sin to skip the "test drive." Customers *rarely* buy cars they don't first drive.)

"Not necessary. I just want your best price." He added that if he liked the price, he'd buy it. If not, he wouldn't. That simple.

Feeling an invisible clock ticking on our exchange (a sensation that should always be present when you're selling to a NOW person), I said, "We can do two things at once." I told him that I would "run" inside and get the process of pulling the invoice on this particular vehicle started. Rather than have him "wait" (something the NOW person is allergic to) for me to figure the best price, I told him we could take a "short" drive. By the time we returned I would know exactly what I could sell him the car for. He acquiesced. (Literally every suggestion coming out of your mouth when dealing with a NOW person should be one of action. You want to speak *his* language.)

In this particular example, the negotiation was simplified by the fact that he didn't have a trade-in and didn't need a payment plan worked out since he would be paying for the car with a (Fortune 100) company check. I offered him a price that incorporated fleet discounting (a discount typically offered to business customers who buy large fleets of vehicles in a short period of time). "Okay," he said. "We have a deal on that one. *Now*, let's see what you can do for me in finding a good little, inexpensive car that my daughter in college can drive for a couple of years."

As we went back out to the lot, he told me how he liked to "kill two birds with one stone." By the time we had finished, I had sold him two cars.

In the end, he was indeed a "fleet customer." He purchased six cars from me in two years!

Here's an instance of what *not* to do with a NOW customer. A real-estate agent I know was commiserating with me about an experience she had with a NOW client who was in the market for a house. Apparently, the client had called in response to a particular house; she had seen the agent's sign in the front yard. After offering the woman some particulars about the house over the phone, the agent attempted to obtain an appointment for viewing the home. The client responded by saying she didn't want to carve time out of her busy day to see only one home. "Have two more in that same subdivision lined up and I can give you one hour after work tomorrow."

"Shopping for a house takes time," the agent cautioned. "We can see this one tomorrow and then set up an appointment when you have more time to look at others," she suggested (or shall I say lectured).

The client, unsatisfied, begged off. The appointment never happened. But the worst part about the real-estate agent's misstep was that she believes to this day she had done the right thing in attempting to "educate" the NOW lady. She felt that it was pointless to waste her time with clients who couldn't give her enough time to do her job right.

I understand the real-estate agent's point. No salesperson likes feeling rushed and dictated to. But the reality is that the only road to a sale with a NOW person is the one where you can speed ahead and skip the rest stops. You have to go at their pace, or you don't go at all.

With a NOW passion–style person, the following phrases can help you to try to guide them through the sales process:

- "Here's the bottom line . . ."
- "I'm proposing this action because . . ."
- "I suggest we do . . ."

**The FASHION CONSCIOUS passion style.** This is typically the customer who cares a great deal about how they look to others. They also like to be made to feel important. In my business, a FASHION CONSCIOUS passion–style customer views a car in terms of their own appearance. "This color will command respect," they will say to themselves when looking at exterior paint color charts.

The FASHION CONSCIOUS passion–style person tends to be influential with others, largely because they *do* care so much and are therefore so driven to be people-pleasers. Think about it. If someone's driving force in life is to make good impressions on others, somewhere along the way they're probably doing just that. They consciously set out to "make connections." They do favors for others and consequently gain favor along the way.

How can you tell when you're dealing with someone with a FASHION CONSCIOUS passion style? Sometimes a person's profession offers clues. A district sales manager for a cosmetics company purchased a car from one of my dealerships the other day. A very well-made-up woman, she was very obviously motivated by how she looked. The popularity and look of the model she bought was more important to her than its crash-test ratings.

My strategy with a FASHION CONSCIOUS passion–style person is to give them a lot of space to shine in the transaction. Compliment them on their taste or way of thinking or anything else you sincerely admire.

FASHION CONSCIOUS passion–style people, because they are social creatures, tend to like to talk a lot. To keep the sales process going in the right direction, it's important to resist conversational detours brought about by their entertaining ways. But be careful not to embarrass them with an interruption. I have found that if I ask them if I *may* interrupt, they're very accommodating.

With a FASHION CONSCIOUS passion–style person, I have found that these kinds of approaches work particularly well:

- "May I have your permission to . . ."
- "How do *you* see . . ."
- "I like the way you . . ."

**The RIGHT passion style.** You've heard the old saws "never argue with a customer" and "the customer is always right." Well, with a RIGHT passion–style person, you never, never argue; they are always, always right. In my business, they typically set out to buy a car only after they have performed much research on their own. They start by researching the car online, reading all the car-related magazines and *Consumer Reports*, and then they comparison-shop various dealerships. They live by very high standards and make use of much analysis to get there.

My strategy with a RIGHT passion–style person? Offer them key details (more data) to support the pro (vs. con) side of the scale.

The real-estate agent I mentioned earlier who butted heads with the NOW passion–style client is certainly a RIGHT passion–style person. She felt like she would be shortchanging her client by taking shortcuts in the viewing of homes. The problem was that her client thrived on taking shortcuts in life. The agent was speaking one language and the client was speaking another. In sales, to communicate on the same wavelength, you have to speak with *their* passion in mind, not yours.

With a RIGHT passion–style person, I find the following phrases effective:

- "Here's a finding . . ."
- "The solution I've identified is . . ."
- "Observe that . . ."

**The STATUS QUO passion style.** I have encountered more STATUS QUO passion–style people than probably all of the other three categories put together. They are the worker bees of our world. They thrive on appreciation. They are loyal, patient, and, as their name implies, steady. The challenge in selling to a STATUS QUO passion–style person—whether you're selling a new car or a new idea—is that they are somewhat resistant to change. And buying something does bring about change—particularly a major purchase such as a home or a car. My strategy with a STATUS QUO passion–style person? Offer them information that helps them understand the *benefits* of change.

Once, when selling to a STATUS QUO passion–style person,

I had to show him why it was worth it to him to have a higher car payment. He had been accustomed to paying $300 per month; the new car he was interested in would raise his payments to $330 per month. What he didn't appreciate at first was that with a new loan, he wouldn't have to begin making payments for sixty days. In essence, he could skip two monthly payments. I pointed out that if he put those two car payments ($600) into his savings account, he could withdraw from it or transfer $30 to his checking account for twenty months to make up the difference between what he was used to paying and the new payment. In other words, for almost the first two years of the loan, the new monthly payment would be the same, making the new loan more pain-free.

I also noted that because he'd be driving a car under warranty (his old one was not), he wouldn't be faced with costly repair bills for quite some time. And the gas mileage was better on the new car than on his, so his fuel costs would be reduced. I took pains to point out the hidden benefits of owning a new vehicle, benefits he might not have seen or appreciated, to help him make the best decision for him. This sales process led to a sale—and a very pleasant one at that.

Often, I can tell what moves someone within minutes of meeting them. This is frequently the case with a STATUS QUO passion–person. In many cases, the manner in which they dress offers early clues. A man dressed in a monochromatic color scheme with a military haircut is often someone who doesn't care to take risks. He might very well be motivated in life by a desire to "maintain" his current situation—that is, to keep things unchanged.

With a STATUS QUO passion–style person, I have found

that the following phrases work best to explain the benefits in a manner they can best understand and appreciate:

- "To minimize the change . . ."
- "I appreciate you for . . ."
- "Let's stay with . . ."

## 13.3 Living with Your Own Passion Style

Let me share with you a recent experience of mine where determining a customer's passion style, and then appealing to it, made the buying and selling process not only easy but also fun for both of us.

In this case, *I* was the customer visiting a boutique in Los Angeles. I needed an after-five dress for an evening function I was not prepared for. After the initial greeting, the saleslady asked me, "Are you looking for something for a wedding?" The only clue she had at the time was that I was headed toward the rack of evening dresses.

"No," I said. "I'm stressing a bit about a function tomorrow night. It's an important event, and I'm totally unprepared. I really want to look my best."

"You're already so beautiful, this is going to be easy," she said reassuringly.

Her opening question (about attending a wedding) gave her all the information she needed to start talking my language— that of a FASHION CONSCIOUS passion–style person who was keenly interested in how she looked to others. (The way I seemed to radiate in response to her compliment reaffirmed it for her.)

Before long, she had selected six dresses for us to take to the "best" dressing room ("it has the brightest lighting and biggest mirrors"), and she was encouraging me to "model" them for her. I found myself getting lost in the fantasy of being a fashion model! I left the boutique that day with a new dress, special undergarments for it, *and* the perfect earrings to accessorize it. I knew I'd feel like the queen of the prom at the black-tie event, thanks to her. I felt every dollar spent was worth it.

I am convinced that determining the passion type of a person, and then applying this information to speak their "language," dramatically improves one's ability to persuade and connect with others.

My husband has certainly learned my style. I have learned his. For me, Tim's profession (engineer) was my earliest tip-off, even before our first date. The way he plays golf was my second. (He plays every round exactly by the rules. No mulligans [do-overs] for him.) Yes, he is a RIGHT passion style.

For his birthday I splurged and got him something whose quality I knew he would appreciate—a Rolex watch. For a wedding gift, he gave me the female version of the same watch. We both love them. He speaks of its craftsmanship. I love how beautiful it is, and how important it makes me feel. We've both learned that a difficult communication can be made better if one of us (at least) starts speaking in the language of the other.

### And in the End . . .

I offer two addendums to our discussion of this powerful communication tool.

One: No one can be reduced to one simple category. We all have unique qualities. In addition, some people have a blend of two or more categories. (In the example above about my fashion emergency, I was acting in both a NOW passion style and a FASHION CONSCIOUS passion style when I walked into that boutique looking for a dress.) Some people may behave one way on one day, and another the next time you visit with them. (After all, we all encounter circumstances that affect our moods, which in turn affect our behavior.) And some people will be one way when alone and another way when they're with others. It's important to keep that in mind when communicating with others in a sales capacity, and to be sensitive to the needs of your customer at that time.

It's up to you to pick up on clues and *customize* your presentation to fit each scenario. (To my mind, that's why the people you are selling to are called *custom*ers.)

However, there is one way in which we all fit into a single category. *All of us* want respect and appreciation. When communicating with others, it's important to always convey high levels of both.

■ **Determining a customer's hot button is an important step in any sales process.** Ask questions, and be sensitive to a customer's clues to learn what that hot button is.

■ **Determine what a customer's passion style is, and learn to talk their "language."** It enhances communication and the likelihood of making a sale.

# Chapter 14

# WHAT YOU NEED TO KNOW ABOUT NEGOTIATING

Negotiating is one of the most misunderstood aspects of selling. There's a whole industry—seminars, workshops, tapes, books—designed to teach people how to negotiate to obtain the best jobs, the best real-estate deals, and, of course, the lowest-priced cars. "How to get the upper hand" negotiation training is available in every city, every day. And yet confusion and fears about negotiation persist.

There are a couple of reasons for this. The first is that most people aren't really sure what a true negotiation is; the second is that we approach the subject differently depending on if we are male or female. When you combine those two factors, it's no wonder we have problems negotiating.

Let's start with a definition of what negotiation is *not*. Contrary to popular belief, negotiation is not a way to gain more power or more leverage over someone. It's not a means by which one party tramples over the other to get their way.

One of the reasons people have problems believing that is the way they approach it.

Men tend to look at negotiation as though it's an intense tug-of-war, or arm wrestling, where finally one party gives in. Once, when a sales manager gave me the "best price" I was to present to my customer, he told me, "Go get 'em, Tiger. Nail 'em."

*Get 'em? Nail 'em?* The nice people sitting on the other side of the desk from me weren't the enemy!

Women, on the other hand, approach negotiations defensively, as though the other side is out to get the best of them.

But even though they may view negotiations differently, most men and women are united in their (mistaken) conclusion: A negotiation is a contest where one person wins over the other.

A negotiation is not a contest. It's a communication, one designed to produce progress. Negotiation is a business term for finding a way—for *both* parties to get, if not exactly what they want, something that works for them.

In truth, negotiation is a means by which at least two people enter into a relationship where they present their respective agendas and, in the end, change their positions enough to be compatible with each other. The key word here is *relationship*. And women thrive inside relationships. Provided they face their fears, I believe that women can excel at negotiating, and perhaps even do the men one better.

I know negotiation can be difficult. I, too, once felt fearful about negotiating. I didn't want to appear argumentative or confrontational. I was worried that the other party might think I was unladylike, and if I *won* the argument, that they might not like me. But once I understood what negotiating really was—forging a relationship—I was able to dismiss the fear that I'd have to aban-

don my femininity and goodwill to become an effective negotiator. After all, when progress and harmony are the ultimate goals
of the interaction, there's little fear of looking disagreeable.

In fact, negotiation is the means to bring about an agree-
ment. I learned that charm and femininity were not only
allowed but were actually useful.

That took care of one fear I had about negotiating. But I was
still afraid of appearing ignorant. I didn't want to make a fool of
myself by letting others know what I didn't know. Over time I
learned that the only antidote for ignorance is knowledge. I now
make sure that I show up for all negotiations with a great command of product knowledge. (As a woman in a man's business,
this is especially important.) To this day, whether I'm negotiating a better interest rate for a loan or better terms for a lease,
preparation continues to be one of my self-confidence boosters.
I also draw on my feminine intuition to read people and try to
speak their language.

With my fears in check, I'm able to show up for a negotiation with eagerness and enthusiasm.

As I've said many times throughout this book, if you're alive,
you're selling. And to take it one step further, if you're selling
(and all of us are), you have to learn how to negotiate. After all,
you're the CEO of your life's journey. Good negotiating skills
will help you to make the journey a smooth one.

## 14.1   Negotiation Made Simple

Without specifically referring to it as such, much of what I've
written in the previous chapters pertains to negotiation. Everything from dressing confidently, to being prepared and orga-

nized, to showing up on time (better yet, early), to inviting people to like you is a part of setting the stage for a healthy negotiation. In essence, what you're demonstrating to the other party with these not-so-small details is that you respect them. But then comes the inevitable, the point where—even when a good foundation for a relationship has been established—two parties have different views about a desired outcome. What happens next? Let me share what has worked for me.

First and foremost: *Adhere to a code of honesty, sincerity, and integrity.* I don't just offer this up as a warm and fuzzy notion. It is critical! When you don't know something, admit it. When you've been wrong about something, admit that, too. You can't change someone's position if they don't trust you. Trust is key.

It's no secret—people tend to distrust car salesmen. To meet this challenge directly, shortly after I opened my first dealership I produced a television commercial where I talked directly into the camera and revealed my (true) age, (true) weight, and (true) shoe size to my prospective customers. I knew I needed some way of letting people know up front that I was different from the image they had in their minds of car dealers. Though the commercial ran for only a short time ten years ago, people still comment (positively) on it. I've been thinking about doing another version of it, even though I'm now a decade older and ten pounds heavier. (Oh well, my shoe size is still the same.)

Assuming you're negotiating from a foundation of high integrity, here are some basic principles to help you turn the wheels of progress:

*Offer refreshments and snacks to break the ice.* As a woman, this is an easy one to me, but it's often overlooked. When I was selling cars, I kept an ice chest full of cold beverages in my office to offer my customers. The drinks came from my private stock. (To this day, I don't like vending machines—they're too impersonal.) A bowl of beautiful red apples on my desk spoke to my desire to nurture my customers. And, of course, I kept boxes of animal crackers in a desk drawer for certain kinds of parental "rescues." This little touch advanced many a negotiation.

*Invite the customer to state* their *position.* You'll never know how close you and your customer are to a desired result unless you ask them in the beginning to tell you what they want. Before I had a customer's car appraised by the manager in charge, I would simply ask, "How much do *you* feel your trade-in is worth?" Occasionally, I would learn that their number was right in line with what our management felt the car was worth.

If they decline to tell you what they want up front, that's fine. There's no magic to who offers the first number, despite what you may have read elsewhere. When a customer of mine refrained from answering my question, I would assure them that I would try to obtain as much as I could for their car, but that I needed their help. I would ask them to share information with me about their car's maintenance records or anything else that might speak to the car's value. Had it been involved in an accident? Were they the original owner? Such information enhanced my knowledge of the product I was selling to *my* management, and it showed the customer that I cared.

Remember, as a negotiator, your responsibility is to achieve harmony. To do that, you need to know what the other party wants or expects. It's hard to do that if your ego gets stuck in who should talk first.

*Present your offer pleasantly but without apology.* I once had an employee come into my office to ask for a raise. Before she had asked for anything, she started apologizing for what she wanted. You can be nice to others without demeaning yourself. People will respect you more. My employee would have been better off coming in enthusiastically and confidently, prepared to state her case and offer her ideas for the betterment of the department.

Another time I heard a car salesman tell a customer, "Before I give you this price, let me say I'm sorry you missed our sale on this model last week." In my book, unless he was in a position to extend the sale offer, there was no point in mentioning it. What good did it do either one of them? It only made the customer feel bad.

*Present your offer and wait patiently for a reply.* Once you've presented your offer, it's good manners to allow the other party time to digest your offer. If you jump the gun and ask, "What do you think?" you're in effect invading their space to think.

*When the other party is frozen, ask them, "What is preventing you from . . . ?"* Sometimes, after presenting an offer to a customer, you get nothing in response: No counteroffer. No objection. No reaction. It's tough to move a person who's frozen. I have learned that asking a question such as "What is preventing you from . . . ?" can help draw them out and help them to verbalize their concerns. Sometimes I hear responses like, "I need to look at cars with lower sticker prices," or "I can't go through with this until I pay off my credit cards," or "I'd feel better if my wife were here." In each case, I was in a position to respond with a helpful suggestion, or even a possible solution.

Do not undermine your position out of desperation. One salesman, after presenting an offer on a car and being met with a customer's blank stare, said, "Would it help you if I could bring the price down?" Effectively, he started negotiating with himself.

*Use exact numbers.* When you use round numbers, you're implying a "general vicinity" price. If you're truly stretching to meet a customer's desired price, give them an exact price. For example, I've never seen a used car that was worth $10,000 that wasn't worth $10,025 or $9,965. And a house that is selling for $200,000 can most certainly be presented for $198,850.

*Proceed with assumptions.* We've all heard that making assumptions in business can be a very dangerous thing. I contend that assumptions have a very legitimate place in negotiations. After all, if you believe your deal is fair, why shouldn't you assume a client does as well? A real-estate agent I know says that when she gets the sense that a customer is happy with the house she's just shown them, she automatically *assumes* they want to make an offer on it, and *assumes* they're willing to pay the asking price. Now, that might seem a bit far-fetched. But as a result, she gets more "asking prices" than any other colleague in her office. Why? Because she assumes she will and that becomes evident in everything she does or says.

Sure, clients not infrequently voice either an inability or unwillingness to pay the seller's asking price. But that enables her to ask the obvious: "How much *are* you comfortable offering?" And as a result, she is much further along in the sales process than her peers would be.

*Think of your product as a "puppy."* I recall the time I allowed my sons to have one of their friend's puppies spend the night. Ten years later, he was still spending the nights with us. Once someone has taken even temporary possession of a product, it's hard to relinquish it. That's why I have established a system for overnight test drives in my dealerships. When a customer says they have to "sleep on it," suggest they sleep *with* it. I've learned that a car is like a puppy dog. Once the kids (or the spouse) have taken a liking to it, and once the neighbors have seen it, it becomes a member of the family.

Ask yourself if your product can be a "puppy dog." I know one enterprising saleslady who sells industrial equipment to petrochemical plants. She delivers new products to her customers for their inspection, whereas her competitors mail brochures.

*Know when to part friends.* There are times when you've taken your case as far as you can and the sale does not go through. Maybe the price the customer expects to pay for your product is unrealistic. Maybe a client has the desire but not the wherewithal to buy. Let it go. Don't let your frustrations or animosity set in. Part friends—they may come back at another time or place in their lives.

I recall one occasion when I stood up from behind my desk and told the customers before me that I thought a bit of continued car shopping would lend credibility to what I had been trying to do for them. That alone seemed to turn the trick.

"Okay," said the husband. "I guess I'm convinced we have a good deal." I went on to wrap up the sale.

I saw a program on "haggling" the other day (how I hate that word), teaching people to "walk away" to get a better deal. I personally have never chased after anyone, and I would never expect to be chased after. If I propose a thanks-anyway ending to the negotiation, I'm genuinely prepared to end the negotiation. If you do initiate a parting of ways, make sure it's sincere and not simply a ploy. (This is true in personal relationships, too.)

## 14.2    Learn What Works for *You*

I'm grateful to my male mentors who made great sacrifices to explain to me the intricacies of the sales profession over the course of my career. Many of my sales managers stayed late to help me close a sale. My colleagues—especially in the beginning of my career—invested a lot of their time teaching me about the products I was selling and how to sell them. I have learned a ton from them. Thank you, guys. You know who you are.

But they taught me what worked for *them*. And being a woman meant I had to discover things for myself. I never knew any other women in car sales. Absent female role models, I experimented and learned what advantages I had as a woman. I negotiated in a way that was contrary to some of the male teachings. Not only did I get away with it, I excelled! In every sales, sales management, or CEO position I have held, I have broken the sales records previously set by men.

Since then, I have passed my unconventional wisdom on to my sales staff (both genders), conference attendees, business audiences, and seminar students. They have used it to discover what works for them, as well.

Here are a few things I learned to do differently:

*1. Be enthusiastic.* We've all heard the advice to "keep a poker face" in negotiations. Whenever I hear or read that expression, I cringe. At best, it implies that as a salesperson you're playing a game. At worst, it suggests you have something to hide. Negotiation isn't a matter of win-and-lose or hide-and-seek. It's a way for at least two parties to advance toward a better position than they were at before. I believe a person's natural enthusiasm can be their greatest asset in sales. After all, an unlit candle can't light another one.

For women, this is where our natural ability to express (rather than rein in) our emotions comes into play. Buying is a very emotional experience. And conversely, I will argue, so is selling. Taking possession of something new (particularly major purchases) should be exciting. It changes your life to some degree. And change is a good thing. Without it there would be no progress or growth. Selling is what turns the wheels of commerce to bring about progress and growth. I think of emotions in selling as grease for the wheels. That's why I feel good when I sell something. And I'm not afraid to show my passion for sales during the entire process!

*2. Never underestimate a "nonbuyer."* Most books on selling recommend that you make sure you're negotiating with the *real* buyer. This has been an area of real opportunity for me in my businesses, because most car salesmen assume that if a woman is in a car dealership alone, they should refrain from any serious negotiations with her because she does not have the authority to make a decision on her own. Well, one policy I have instituted in my dealerships is that women be taken very seriously as customers.

Even if it's true that a wife is gathering information to take home to discuss with her husband, I never minimize her influence in the final buying decision.

Similarly, I remind my sales staff that it's important to treat customers who can't buy a car because of poor credit with the same kind of respect you would offer someone who is able to write a check for one. First of all, respect should be nondiscriminating. It also makes good business sense. My experience has taught me that people who *can't* buy have friends and relatives who *can*. I continue to receive an abundance of referrals from nonbuyers. (And, of course, as their credit improves, they, too, may become a customer.)

3. *If you can live with the first offer, take it.* The generally accepted wisdom is that a salesperson never accepts a first offer because it shows he or she is weak. I strongly disagree. Sometimes accepting a first offer shows you're smart. I don't believe in "going back and forth" just for the exercise. The one time I failed to take my own advice, I lost out. I made an offer on a house I had always dreamed of owning, and the seller made a very modest, reasonable counteroffer. Rather than take their first response, I countered back. Somewhere in the process, someone else came along and offered the seller the full asking price with a check in hand. My dream house suddenly disappeared. Negotiating is more than splitting the difference. Besides possibly losing out, you can waste time and erode goodwill. If you're like me, you're out to succeed for the long haul. It's much more likely for a customer to return to you the next time around if you didn't pin them to the mat, so to speak. And I'd much rather sit down with that person negotiating from a spirit of gratitude than one of "get even."

In the end, being at a negotiation table is a privileged position. It means someone wants and needs your help. You get to help someone—and help yourself at the same time. It's about striking a chord of harmony. And harmony doesn't cost. It pays.

■ **There is nothing to be scared about.** If you think about negotiation as a way of cultivating a relationship, as opposed to some winner-take-all fight to the death, most of your concerns about negotiation will disappear.

■ **Be honest and fair, and seek common ground.** It seems so basic, but you'd be amazed how often people don't do this. Yet they are surprised when the negotiation doesn't go well.

■ **If you're a woman, you don't have to negotiate like a man.** There is no need to use a poker face or to squeeze every last nickel out of the deal. Remember: You are trying to forge a relationship, not win a war.

# Chapter 15

# DEALING WITH DIFFICULT PEOPLE

I n a perfect world, all of your customers would be reasonable, fair people. But, of course, customers aren't always nice. They're not always reasonable. "Fair dealing" is something that many of them have no concept of.

I once heard a customer service manager for a large department store say that she "specialized" in difficult people. That's great for the other employees in her department store, but few salespeople have the luxury of pushing off a difficult customer onto someone else. The reality is that all successful salespersons learn how to deal with difficult people. Whenever I hear salespeople on my staff complain about how unreasonable a customer is, I remind them: *None of us has the luxury of selling only to nice people.*

What differentiates a routine (order-taker) salesperson from a great one is his or her willingness and ability to deal with tough customers. A real-estate agent once told me, "I'm here to help clients *if* they want to buy. But if a client needs to be sold, they can go down the road." From my perspective, she would be better off taking her "if" into another profession. As harsh as that may sound, those of us who have been successful in sales understand that the job involves more than just greeting people who know exactly what they want to buy. We have to work for our earnings (that's why they're called *earn*ings), and sometimes that means dealing with people who engage in less-than-desirable behavior. But there is no better feeling than knowing that we were able to soften (a "girl" word, I know) a tough, contentious client or customer—at least long enough to make the sale. A huge part of the reward that comes from sales is in surmounting the challenges we face every day. And there is no bigger challenge than difficult people.

## 15.1  A Few One-Size-Fits-All Approaches

There are as many approaches to handling difficult people as there are different kinds of difficult people. Accordingly, I've organized the material below to fit particular challenges. But I want to begin by offering a few universal principles.

First, it's important to remember that *customers in tough situations need to feel supported.*

This is another area where I believe women have an advantage. Many a proud man refers to himself as a "Mr. Fix-it," someone who can get a problem solved. And that's a good thing. Customers do need solutions. If they come to you with a problem, they certainly want it taken care of. But they also need to feel *supported.* Most women understand the difference between providing a solution for a customer and offering them support.

Recently, I "visited" (that's what I call coaching sessions with my employees) with one of my male service advisers. He had a female customer who came in complaining of a rattling sound coming from under the hood of her brand-new car. He wrote up the repair order and proceeded to have the car fixed. The job was completed, the rattle was eliminated, and the car was delivered back to the customer on time. And since the job was under warranty, there was no charge to the customer. So, to the service adviser, all seemed well.

When I told him that the customer had turned in a less-than-satisfactory customer survey (we send them out to everyone who has done business with us), he expressed shock. "Her car was fixed when she drove off!" He went on, "I believe she's being unfair."

I explained that he had provided the customer with a solution; the woman had no problem with the repair. But he had not offered her a show of support. He would have been better served to listen for more than the sound coming from under the hood. She was crying out for her service adviser to offer her assurances that the expensive car she had just purchased was still a good choice, that he cared about her problem, and that he would be there for her whenever she needed help. He took care of the car but not the customer. That wasn't enough from the customer's point of view. And that is the only point of view that matters.

This example suggests another general principle I've discovered about appeasing challenging customers: *Customers in tough (at least for them) situations need empathy.*

Chances are better than good that this particular customer's day had been disrupted by her car problem. But her pain was never acknowledged by her service adviser (who's a good guy, and now, I promise, wiser for the experience). She needed to hear him *say* that he felt bad for her. An expression of empathy might have caused her to vent a bit, but at least she would have felt better afterward. As it was, she vented her feelings of neglect by giving him derogatory marks on the survey. When the service manager (the service adviser's immediate supervisor) called her—upon receipt of the survey—he expressed all that the service adviser should have told her from the start. (He also thanked her for her input.) Hopefully, with our early response to the survey, she didn't feel the need to speak negatively about our dealership to anyone else.

That brings up a point. As I've said before, referral and repeat business are the keys to long-term success. Happy customers come back. They tell their friends and families where to buy their cars. As a salesperson, you need to understand that challenging—and even unfair—people talk, too, sometimes more than most people. And their listeners hear only one version of the story (theirs). That's another reason to find a way to satisfy *all* of your customers, including those who are difficult.

## 15.2    Sometimes, You Just Have to Laugh

I take what I do for a living seriously, but I try not to take myself that way. My third general principle is: *Keep, and (when appropriate) use, your sense of humor.*

I have learned over the years that there is usually some humor to be found in even the most difficult of situations. (I recall my mom, visiting me in the hospital, reaching into her pocket for a Kleenex to wipe her tears when I was diagnosed with cancer. Her Kleenex was a $10 bill! We both broke out laughing, and still laugh about it to this day.) Humor can help to defuse a tense situation.

A good sense of humor can also help to cushion sales rejection. And that's important, because it prevents us from bringing unnecessary baggage from one sales transaction to another. It wouldn't be fair to greet a new customer with distrust because the previous customer treated you badly. Self-effacing humor can help to clean the slate.

Let me give you an example. One morning, I suffered three "no-shows" in a row. By one o'clock, I needed to get out of my office for a while, so I invited a colleague, who knew of my frustrating morning, to lunch. "Today I'm buying," I said. "Given all of the money I've made this morning, it's only fair." We both laughed.

A breath of fresh air, a nice lunch, and a few laughs later, I was back at work eager to greet my three o'clock appointment. (They showed, and I made a sale.) That is the power of humor.

Principle number four: Don't take a customer's rudeness or wrath personally. The minute you do, you've given away power: Your power to think clearly. Your power to improve the situation. And your power to make the sale.

When I was first applying for a job as a car salesman, the manager I was interviewing with told me he had "never considered a *woman* for a sales management position." I realized that his comment was more a statement about him than about me. By not taking his remarks to heart, I was able to open up his way of thinking and show him the benefits of hiring a woman (e.g., I would be more nurturing with and be better able to train the sales staff). By remaining *present* and in command of myself, instead of mentally running off and becoming defensive, my *presenta*tion stayed intact. If I had attacked him for making such a (stupid) statement, I would have been proving his point—that a woman was too emotional for the job. And I would have lost the job.

The moment you take another person's unfairness or obnoxiousness personally, you risk losing yourself. Don't lose your head when you need it most.

## 15.3    Specific Approaches for Tough Characters

As I've said throughout the book, selling any product or service to a person is about helping them. But how do you go about helping someone who seems to be looking for a fight, or claims to know it all already (and so contends he or she doesn't need help)? How do you please someone who seems to take pleasure in the very act of complaining?

None of us wants to be somebody's punching bag. But there are ways to calm someone and move even stubborn people down the path toward a successful sale. But before I offer my servings of "how to's," let me offer an important disclaimer.

*Never* put yourself in harm's way by trying to persuade someone who is truly deranged. We once had a man enter the showroom demanding to see me, telling the receptionist that he had a gun in his pocket. I was alerted, the police were called, and he was very quickly apprehended. It turns out that he did have a gun, as well as a criminal record. He had picked me as his target because I reminded him of his ex-wife!

I would have been foolish had I tried to persuade him to be reasonable. You can't make sense of insanity. So don't try.

But other than extreme cases like that, if you want to make a living in sales, avoiding difficult customers is not an option. So let's talk about what you should do.

## MR. STONE FACE

I lightly touched on this customer in the chapter on negotiation. But Mr. Nonresponsive deserves to be included here, as well. He's truly difficult. He doesn't give you much to work with, because he shows no emotion. The temptation on the part of the salesman is to shake him and blurt out, "Tell me what you want." But it wouldn't do any good. Typically, he or she is as hard as a rock.

On a car lot, a typical Mr. Stone Face won't say much. Nor does his body language reveal much. He kind of follows along— looking down at the ground, maybe kicking a pebble or two— occasionally giving his salesperson a nod or a hint of a small smile.

Making a sale to a customer who gives you so little to work with doesn't come easy.

First, assume he doesn't trust you. Or anyone. But remember not to take it personally. This is about him. Maybe he got ripped off the last time he bought whatever it is you're selling. Maybe he's distrustful of everyone. It doesn't matter. You've got to earn his trust, even though you didn't lose it.

Tell him something about yourself that shows *you* trust *him*. (It may sound bizarre, but it's an approach I've used more than a few times successfully.) Trust is the basis for all healthy transactions or relationships, and it has to begin somewhere. With a "stone face," it needs to begin with you. The beauty is that trust breeds trust. Once "stone face" starts to trust you, he'll begin to see that maybe you're okay after all, and start to open up—a bit.

Last, as you open up to such a customer, it's important to remember to use your softest tone of voice, and to reveal yourself in terms of *feelings*. When you do both of these things, you're subliminally guiding your customer toward their own emotions and inviting them to reach out to you. Before I begin to sound too off-the-wall, let me tell you about a time when I did exactly this.

I had managed to get as far as to learn that my customer, the quintessential Mr. Stone Face, was "in the market" for a four-door, midsize, new car. Getting that much out of him had been like pulling teeth. But my attempts to learn anything else about him or his needs were met with "It depends" or "I'm not sure" or a muffled mumble. I was unable to get him to select any particular car, let alone discuss pricing and other pertinent matters.

Assuming that he had some apprehensions about the whole process of buying a car, I told him that the nicest thing about my profession was that as long as I was in it, I never had to be in his position, shopping for a car. "Speaking for myself, I'd dread doing what you're doing now," I said. "I'm easily swayed, so I'd be afraid."

And miracle of miracles, my stone-faced customer responded in kind: "The only reason I even have to do this is because my wife got *my* car in the divorce," he told me. With the one comment, it seemed that the dam broke! He went on to tell me how unjust the terms of the divorce had been, how "weak" his attorney was, and how unfair the judge had been. I offered support ("Will your ex-wife, at least, have to pick up the payments on what used to be your car?") and empathy ("I feel for you"). And in the end, I was able to provide him with a solution: a new car that belonged only to him.

Thinking back on it later, my being a woman (the same gender as his wife) was probably a factor contributing to his closed persona. I'm glad I never took his behavior personally.

## THE ETERNAL FRAT BOY

I suppose being a woman qualifies me to speak on this subject. I have had plenty of "passes" thrown my way, and I've never won any beauty contests. I've chosen to handle remarks from male customers in a way that brings them back to earth. These "cowboys" (I'm from Texas) get the loop of my lasso, you might say. (If you've ever been to a rodeo, you've seen how a rider sits on a galloping horse, swinging a large looped rope around and around above his head, aiming for a calf he's chasing. Once he's gotten close enough to the calf to put the loop—lasso—around the calf, the chase comes to a halt.)

Let me give you an example.

"How did you like the way the car handled?" I asked a customer after we got back to the dealership from a test drive.

"I couldn't concentrate on the car because I was looking at your legs," he shot back.

Rather than taking his remark personally, I deflected it to my advantage. "Thank you," I told him. "Now why don't you let my legs go to work for you? Let's go inside and wrap up the deal." Inside we went. He told me later that he liked how "tough" I was.

Please don't misunderstand me. I do not condone bad behavior. You should never subject yourself to any kind of harassment. But I've found that there are times when deflecting a fresh remark and using it to your advantage can help you make a sale.

### THE KNOW-IT-ALL

I recall negotiating with a very intelligent computer science engineer long before the Internet pierced the veil of industry secrets. He opened his hard metal briefcase with such seriousness that one might have thought he was carrying a formula for biological warfare. Out came a scroll about three feet long bearing his calculations for the "dealer's cost" of his desired minivan. After examining his work, I found that his numerical gyrations had come within four cents of the actual manufacturer's invoice. "Very good work," I proclaimed, and I meant it. He had done his homework. Now what?

Without even realizing it, I had done a good thing. I had validated what he had done. Here was a guy whose obsession in life was about being right. (Recall the passion styles discussed earlier?) But then I took a wrong turn.

I proceeded to make my case for the dealership making a little bit of money on the sale, and how profit wasn't a dirty word. "No business can survive if all it's able to do is cover its overhead," I pointed out. "Your figures don't reflect all of the costs involved in the selling of this minivan. We've paid interest on it and insurance and advertising and . . ." In essence, I was arguing my case by putting his down, and thereby putting him down. Wrong move!

He repacked his briefcase and stood up, telling me that I hadn't heard him out. He was prepared to offer me a "reasonable profit." But I never got to hear what it was. I had gotten sidetracked making a case instead of a sale.

With a know-it-all customer, never get in an "I know more" contest. For you to win, they have to lose. And someone who's just been made to feel like a loser doesn't feel like buying any-thing. So what have you won?

Instead of taking them head-on, offer key details to support their case.

With my computer science engineer, I would have been much better off discussing how helpful his research was. "The work you've done has made my job easier. Here are a few more costs to be aware of—the interest, insurance, and advertising the dealership paid on the minivan." Chances are, had I invited him, he would have given these costs to the dealership their due consideration. It took me a few botched sales with "know-it-alls" for me to learn this essential lesson. Now I *know*.

## MS. INDECISIVE

I confess; I'm doing a bit of stereotyping by naming this charac-ter "Ms." But we women have long and proudly proclaimed our prerogative to change our minds. Even for the best people in sales, fickle and indecisive customers are challenging. "It's like you've got a moving goal line," a male colleague once told me after dealing with a particularly indecisive customer. I don't dis-agree.

In a day and age when women are struggling to balance com-peting priorities, you'd think we'd be more decisive if for no other reason than to save time. But in fact, the opposite is true. The decision-making process can actually take longer, because we can't afford the time to focus on it. And so we often defer it.

Keeping that in mind, the most important piece of advice I can offer is: *Be patient.* Hurried, stressed-out customers don't like to be pressured or rushed.

But being patient doesn't mean you should do nothing. While there's no magic wand you can wave to help someone make up their mind, there are a few things you can do that are helpful.

For starters: *Present the idea of owning your product in a way that minimizes risk to your customer.* I've come to learn that people who have difficulty making up their minds often equate decision making with gambling. They need to be made to feel that they have little or nothing to lose. Talking up the benefits of ownership isn't enough.

A real-estate agent I know learned that the hard way:

"I had weeks invested with a female client who kept changing her mind about everything from her preference of subdivisions to her budgeted price range. Only after experiencing as much disappointment and frustration as I felt I could endure, I told her that she might be better off working with another agent. She took my advice and chose a colleague in my firm. Within twenty-four hours of their meeting, I saw her in his office signing an offer for him to submit to a seller! Well, I couldn't resist. When I saw her leaving, I congratulated her on being able to finally find a house that suited her and asked her what about this house made her make the move. 'I liked a couple of the houses you showed me better, but this one is a good investment. I don't feel like I'd have to live there the rest of my life,' she told me. I felt like a lightbulb suddenly went on. Where I had been focusing on square footage, flooring, and amenities in the homes (benefits), my colleague stressed what she needed to hear the most—her purchase was safe."

The "decision making is like gambling" theory also explains why indecisive people seem to solicit opinions of so many others. They need assurances from people they trust. It's important that you respect their needs. Even after you have done your best to minimize the risks associated with buying, *give indecisive customers space to include the opinions of others.*

"I can't make a decision until I get my ex-husband's opinion," a woman once told me.

"May I give you some privacy so that you can phone him?" I responded. She did just that, and he gave her the nod. In essence, he made the sale for me. Her case is extreme, but it makes the point. Customers are often reluctant to take the plunge of ownership until they can be assured by someone in their trusted inner circle that they're doing the right thing. In extreme cases, I've been known to ask a customer, "Is there someone we can call whose opinion you value?" (But use this sparingly; it can backfire. On one occasion when I suggested it to a young female divorcée, she answered, "That's a good idea. I think I'll put off shopping for a car until I go home for Christmas. That way my dad can go with me.")

The point is, *never* discourage or ridicule a customer's need to get opinions from others. You can't—nor should you—talk people out of reaching for help. I once heard a salesman (not one of my employees) say to a potential customer who wanted to talk to their best friend before making the purchase decision, "Who's going to be making the payments on this car? You or your friend?" Bad move. By putting it that way, he caused his customer to feel defensive. And people don't typically buy from someone they view as offensive.

And last: *Refrain from using the word "why."* "Why" is a word that keeps people stuck. When you ask someone why they feel like they do, you're inviting them to reinforce the negatives. Let's say you don't agree with your significant other on an issue. If you ask him why he feels like he does, chances are he'll tell you, and by doing so, he's actually reinforcing his belief.

Asking a customer why they can't make up their mind has the same effect. Their doubt becomes stronger. Instead, try a phrase such as "*What's* preventing you from . . . ?" Their answer to this question doesn't invite them to make a long, drawn-out case for not moving forward, but rather to voice a specific objection. (Once you know what it is, of course, you're in a position to address it.)

And as a footnote, let me say that over the years it has been my experience that while women are slower at making their buying decisions, in the end, they are the most loyal. They tend to make up a disproportionate percentage of repeat customers. It's the relationship thing again. Women value relationships, plain and simple.

## THE HOTHEAD

I've seen more than a few hotheads in my time. No car owner is happy about their automobile breaking down. But some customers get hotter than their overheated engine. It's tough to deal with someone who's demonstrating an extremely low level of rationality. But it can be done.

First and foremost, keep *your* cool. Having raised two sons, I draw on my experience as a mother. Screaming and yelling wouldn't have done me any good then, when my three-year-old was throwing a fit because he didn't get his way, and it wouldn't do any good now in dealing with (supposedly) more mature adults. The key is to stay calm, cool, and collected.

In my early days as a car dealer, I received one too many

complaints about a service manager who had a difficult time with this principle. Shouting matches were almost a sport to him. Needless to say, his tenure was very short-lived. I have never seen an exchange of tempers solve a problem, let alone sell a product.

But how do you go about reasoning with a customer who is out of control? Earlier, I discussed the importance of showing support and empathy with challenging customers. The person who's demonstrating open anger needs a double dose of both. As difficult as it may sound, it's the only road to reasoning with this person. Until you administer support and empathy, they won't be able to hear a thing you say. Let me give you an example.

A female loan officer for a local bank called my office one morning, saying that my finance manager had misrepresented some information about a customer on a credit application that she had approved. She insisted to my secretary that she see me "TODAY."

My secretary scheduled an appointment for later that afternoon, which allowed me the time to conduct an internal investigation.

When the loan officer entered my office, I offered her a beverage, which she turned down. "I didn't come here to socialize," she all but snarled.

I took a seat next to her on the same side of the desk (a showing of support) and listened as she told her story. When she wound down, I told her that I valued our relationship with her and the bank she represented. "I am very supportive of your position in this matter," I said. With that, her body language seemed to relax a bit. "You've obviously been put in a very painful situation with this," I empathized. She proceeded to tell me just how painful it was for her, feeling she had been taken advantage of. She also told me her decision had caused her to look bad to the loan committee.

But now it was time for her to hear *my* truth.

"After your call this morning, I delved into the matter to prepare for our meeting. It seems our *customer* misrepresented the information contained on this credit application," I explained. "We didn't catch it either."

From that point forward, I felt as if I were discussing the problem with a totally different person. (She even changed her mind about the beverage.) We not only formulated a remedy for the problem but created preventative measures to ensure that the fiasco could never be repeated.

Support. Empathy. Truth. In that order. I know that had I tried to share the truth with her before offering support and empathy, it would have landed on deaf ears.

---

- **The difference between a sales "clerk" and a sales "pro"** is that the pro actually looks at challenging customer situations as opportunities. The clerk sees them as something to avoid at all costs.
- **Not every customer problem can be solved.** But every customer can be supported. Every customer needs and deserves to be heard.
- **Being patient with difficult customers is the foundation for dealing with them.** Whether a customer's a hothead, a know-it-all, or just indecisive, there are strategies you can use. But they all take a calm presence of mind. Nothing will be accomplished if you are impatient.

# Chapter 16

# REJECTION: HOW TO LEARN FROM IT AND EARN FROM IT

R ejection comes with the territory," a sales manager once told me.

Whether your sales "territory" is a counter or a county, whether you are pitching for extra practice time for your son or a more convenient appointment to see your doctor, we all experience rejection at times. And that brings up an even greater truth: *Rejection's hard for everyone.* After all, if you care about making the sale, it naturally follows that you'll care when you don't make the sale.

Salespeople generally handle rejection in one of two ways. Some, women particularly, tend to internalize rejection. Others externalize it. When a woman comes up empty-handed in a sale, she commonly asks, "What's wrong with me?" or "What did I do wrong?" In essence, she overpersonalizes the event.

Men, on the other hand, tend to ask, "What's wrong with that customer?"

Both responses have an upside and a downside. I know this contradicts the common perception that men deal with rejection better. But the conventional wisdom is wrong. Men deal with rejection differently than women do, but not necessarily better. The truth is we would do well to learn from each other.

Let's examine the negative sides of externalizing and internalizing rejection.

## 16.1    Externalizing Rejection

The problem with looking outside of yourself for an answer to why you were rejected is that you miss an opportunity to examine *your* role in the experience. How can you make adjustments (improvements) to your sales presentation if you never consider what you might do better?

One of my salesmen once complained to me that three customers in a row had "stiffed" him. "I don't know what it is with these people," he said with a sigh. Worried that I would think less of him, he added, "I'll shake it off and get the next one."

"Let's look at what's going on," I coached him. "Perhaps this is more than coincidence." As we talked, we looked at *his* role in the missed sales. He discovered that in each case he had never asked for the order.

"I've been running to each base but have been stopping at third," he suddenly realized. He went on to make changes in his presentation, taking complete charge of the sales process (including the close). And he started enjoying much more success. Had he merely shaken it off, he would have missed out on an opportunity to learn from the best teacher of all—experience.

## 16.2 Internalizing Rejection

The tendency to internalize rejection can be just as detrimental as one's inclination to blame someone else for an inability to make a sale. If we interpret a customer's (or anyone's) decision not to buy as a reflection of something wrong with ourselves, our self-esteem is the casualty. We risk becoming immobilized—stuck in a "what's wrong with me?" or a "why me?" state of mind. To be a successful salesperson, you have to have confidence, you have to believe in yourself. While the externalizer shakes it off and goes full speed (perhaps in the wrong direction but nevertheless in motion), the internalizer can become stuck in the land of "I'm not good enough." It's hard to convince or persuade anyone else of your point of view if you're paralyzed by feeling down.

## 16.3 Taking Charge of Your Feelings

Whether you externalize or internalize rejection, the effects can be toxic. But there is an antidote: *balance*—using an appropriate level of externalizing and internalizing to reset your inner compass.

Allowing yourself to become emotionally paralyzed because of someone else's decision (overinternalizing) is the same as giving away your power. On the other hand, the ability to look in the mirror anytime you've suffered a setback, to ask yourself what you might try to do differently the next time (appropriate internalizing), is empowering. It allows you to be fully present in the experience. And it reminds you that no one can make you feel "less than" without your permission.

What about the external side of the equation? Remind yourself that there are always circumstances beyond your control (appropriate externalizing). I have learned from years of dealing with rejection that recognizing the part my customers, or other circumstances, play in a missed sale (maybe they just weren't ready to buy) helps me to temper my feelings.

The challenge is to refrain from blaming those who you perceive have hurt you (overexternalizing). Blaming a customer for a missed sale weakens *you* for the next sale. Once again, you've given your power away. The customer you're about to greet or call on has no knowledge of your previous rejection. They came to you with a clean slate. You should come to them the same way. There's no worse way to start a sales process than with emotional baggage from a previous experience.

I once had a furniture saleslady ask me to "forgive" her bad mood—the last customer she had had was "impossible." But her brusque attitude toward me wasn't something I could quickly get past.

Remember, you control the way you choose to respond to rejection. You—and only you—can take charge of your response. Be response-*able*. A dose of internalization mixed with externalization can bring balance to your handling of any sales experience. I think of it as the yin and the yang of handling rejection.

## 16.4    Compartmentalizing Your Feelings

As I have said, feeling hurt by rejection is natural. I think of our feelings as internal signals reminding us that we care. If someone you care about jilts you, you hurt. The message from the pain is that you care about the person, and the missed opportunity to make a connection. Your feelings are there to let you know how you are responding to the world around you.

As women, our "feelings antennae" can be especially sensitive, picking up all kinds of signals. Experts comment on our "feminine intuition." (No one speaks of *masculine* intuition.) But speaking as a confessed emotional hemophiliac—someone whose feelings can sometimes flow too freely and visibly—I believe there is a proper time, place, and way to express our feelings. As a result, I've learned to compartmentalize my feelings in order to avoid inappropriately expressing them in front of a client or customer. They can be shared later with my husband or a friend.

For me, this lesson did not come overnight. So my first suggestion is to be patient—with yourself. There are still times when I have to remind myself to tuck my feelings away until later. Remember, I am not suggesting that you ignore them or push them away. Your feelings are part of your uniqueness. Own them—but manage them, so that they don't manage you.

I had been retained by an out-of-state women's business forum to deliver a motivational speech. As a newlywed, I was finding it tough to travel and be apart from my husband, Tim. Nonetheless, I had agreed to do it. To make matters worse, before the trip, Tim and I got "off stride." I felt sad and rejected.

Minutes before going onstage, I was at the point of tears. I took a few deep breaths (always a good idea) and reminded myself that my feelings were a reminder of my love for him. And for now, that was all I needed to deal with.

I refrained from assigning blame. Engaging in self-blame (internalizing the rejection) would have been devastating to my self-esteem at a time I needed to be self-confident. Blaming him (externalizing the rejection) would have angered me and diverted my energy and focus. By resisting the temptation to lay blame, I was able to harness my energy for the task at hand, speaking before the audience who had come to hear me. By compartmentalizing my feelings temporarily, I was able to make the speech a success. And Tim and I were able to address our hurt feelings upon my return that evening.

I should add that by the time I returned home and my husband and I had talked about our miscommunication, I was less upset. That's true of most events that cause us to experience hurt feelings. Nothing seems as bad later as it does at the time it happens—yet another reason to pause before we act on our feelings.

## 16.5  Facing Rejection

I have experienced enough rejection in my life to fill a book, let alone a chapter. I have been stood up for appointments. I have been lied to and betrayed. I have been told no more times than I can count. On occasion, I have been ridiculed and excluded in the workplace. I'll never be able to say I like rejection. But I truly don't fear it anymore.

As I travel all over the world and talk to people about their dreams, what I have come to know is that the biggest drag on most people's lives isn't a lack of knowledge, money, or other wherewithal. It's fear. Fear of change. Fear of failure. And the biggest fear of all? Fear of rejection.

"I've been passed up three times for the promotion I want," a woman told me.

"What has prevented you from coming right out and asking for it?" I asked her.

"What if they say no?" she responded. Her fear of rejection was so severe that it was keeping her stuck. To her, working at a dead-end job, letting the days, months, and years slip by, was preferable to facing the possibility of a no.

In reality, no can be a great friend to us. Here's how I deal with it:

First, I allow myself an appropriate "period of mourning" each and every time I feel rejected. I allow myself to feel the hurt without resisting or denying it. In the midst of it, I call on my sense of resiliency—an attribute I believe is inherent to most women (what man would have a second baby?). My ability to bounce back from the pain of rejection is a constant boost to my self-confidence. Maybe I didn't get what I wanted—the customer said no, or we couldn't come to terms—but I give myself credit for being someone who can bounce back and succeed the next time. I'm someone who thrives on life's possibilities, and as a result, the only failure for me is not trying.

Most times, I am able to analyze my role in a missed opportunity and profit from the experience. I have been a student in my relationships (transactions) even when the other person was unaware they were teaching me. I have looked for ways my failures could lift me up. *Failure is an event, not a person.*

I have found that when I honor my hurt feelings but discipline my behavior, I emerge from the experience stronger and wiser.

■ **Some people externalize rejection; others internalize it.** To be successful, you need to balance what is right in both approaches.

■ **Assume responsibility for hurt feelings, and decide when and how to deal with them.** To be successful in sales takes a willingness to harness hurt feelings without dismissing or giving in to them.

■ **Our fear of rejection can be overcome and replaced with a feeling of empowerment and enhanced self-worth.** But it takes a conscious decision. And it takes courage. It won't just come to you.

# Chapter 17

# 12 SURE WAYS TO AVOID BLOWING A SALE

There are probably as many ways to blow a sale as there are salespeople. But besides the fundamental mistakes—lack of preparation and product knowledge—there are twelve common mistakes even the best salespeople make. If you can avoid them, you'll increase your chances of success exponentially. They are:

**1. Don't lie.** This commandment is *not* negotiable. Trust is the basis for every sound relationship. If you're anything less than honest, it will catch up to you. You will be found out. And the price for being found out is high. Your good reputation will be the first casualty, because people who have been deceived avenge themselves by telling other people about what you've done to them.

Even if deceptive sales tactics seem to bring you success in the beginning, your success will be short-lived, I promise. Speaking as an employer, I can tell you that any salesperson who uses deception as a means to increase sales is not worth the damage he or she causes.

I once terminated a seemingly productive salesman because of just that. In the beginning, I was astonished by his sales performance. Right off the bat, he started outselling even the most veteran people on the floor. But in just a matter of weeks, his lies started to surface.

The finance manager, responsible for helping customers find ways to pay for their new cars, told me his transactions were difficult to process because the customers were often misinformed about matters like taxes, insurance, and titling fees. They had been told that these items were included in the sales price. (They weren't.)

Initially, I believed that the salesman was confused about these matters and hadn't done anything wrong intentionally. Then I began receiving calls from the service manager to okay various expenses generated by promises the salesman had made to his customers. For example, the salesman had told customers that he would include additional or upgraded equipment—full-size spare tires, better sound systems, tinted windows, and so on—at no extra charge. He had thrown them in to clinch the deal and get his commission, unconcerned that those "extras" were coming out of the dealership's profits.

The first couple of incidents, I wrote it off as miscommunication between the customer and the salesman. (I always approved the add-ons.) But then I began to make the connection between the incidents; he was a loose cannon who would say anything to close a deal. Ultimately, I decided he had to go.

I fired him for a number of reasons. Yes, he was hurting our profits and causing me needless stress, and either of those things would have been enough to make my decision. But the main reason I terminated his employment was the impact his lies and deception had on the sales staff. Their morale began to suffer. I had less time to help them, because I was always running around putting out the fires caused by "the new guy." If I kept him on, my other employees would start to think that it was all right to lie to increase sales. I also had to think about the damage he caused to the reputation of the dealership. Customers might tell their neighbors we tried to rip them off when we explained that the terms or options he had promised were not available. His dishonest tactics came at a high price to everyone.

**2. Don't shove them away.** Even when you don't have what a customer is looking for, it's important to offer them help in finding what they need. You'll benefit by knowing that you're helping someone, and by befriending someone who may remember you when they *do* want something you sell. By contrast, if you simply tell them to go "up the street," they'll feel no connection to you or any reason to do business with you in the future.

Let me give you an example. DaimlerChrysler is the manufacturer of both Mercedes and Chrysler vehicles. In the cities where my dealerships are located, I am franchised to sell Chrysler cars but not Mercedes; another dealer sells those. And that sometimes causes confusion.

"My wife wants a new Mercedes," a local businessman told me. After inviting him to test-drive Chrysler's luxury lineup, I realized that what I had to offer was not what she was looking for. "All of her life, she's dreamed of owning a Mercedes," the businessman told me.

So I referred him to a colleague at the local Mercedes dealership who I knew would give him quality customer service. Then

I called the colleague to inquire about the availability of the models the businessman was looking for, and arranged for an appointment for him to visit the dealership.

After going there, the businessman called me back to thank me, telling me that he had been treated well. He ordered a Mercedes that was going to take twelve weeks to come in.

"I've been thinking," he said, "if I were to lease a car like the 300 C Chrysler, it could serve her in the interim, and I could drive it after that. Could you take my car in as a trade-in, but let me keep it until her Mercedes comes in?" I told him yes, and we worked out the details. He ended up being *my* customer, too! I know in my heart that had I offered him a curt "I don't handle Mercedes" when he first came to me, he would never have called me back to report in, much less considered me to meet the rest of his transportation needs.

**3. Don't be rude.** Rude behavior has no place in any sales presentation. But to take it one step further, it has no place in your day. As I've stated before, a salesperson is always "on"—even when you are the customer.

Case in point: I witnessed a lady placing her breakfast order for eggs in a way that caught the attention of every diner in the restaurant. "Runny egg whites gross me out. So make *sure* they're overhard," she barked.

When her breakfast was delivered to her, she took her fork and dramatically started stabbing the eggs, raising her voice to the waitress and demanding, "Do these look hard to you?" The harsh tone and sarcasm she used were painful to listen to. Everyone in the restaurant felt sorry for the waitress; you could see it in the glances they exchanged.

As I exited the restaurant behind this woman, I saw her get

into a car that had a magnetic sign on the door advertising her real-estate agency. Now, you tell me—would you want to buy a house from her?

Rude behavior isn't always so obvious. Sometimes we're rude without realizing it. When you're hurried or intensely focused on something, be careful to listen to what you say and how you respond to interruptions. For example, my husband called me on this one the other day. His phone call came in when I was trying to outrun the clock to prepare for a meeting. "What's up?" I answered as soon as I saw his name on the caller ID and hit the answer button.

"Hey, what happened to hello?" he responded. The time I spent apologizing to him would have been unnecessary had I been nice in the first place.

**4. Don't beg or panic.** As a salesperson, you are charged with being the helper. At no time during the sales process should you be the one asking for help.

A salesman at a men's store told me that if he didn't make his quota for the month, he was going to be let go. I wanted him to let *me* go. For a customer, it's a turnoff to feel obligated to buy something when they're being pressured or made to feel guilty.

There were times when I was but one sale away from earning a bonus or an award (e.g., a fabulous trip). But I instinctively knew never to convey that information to my customers.

When you concentrate on the needs of your customers, your own needs will be fulfilled, too.

**5. Don't get too personal.** Customers are entitled to professionalism from you. At no time should you share information about your life in a way that might make them feel uncomfortable or that detracts from their getting what they want and need. They don't need to know the details of your personal life. That is what friends and family are for.

In my early days of selling, I heard a car salesman tell a customer, "Bear with me. I have an excruciating hangover." (Now, there's a visual.) Could he possibly have believed that information would help them to be more sympathetic to his plight?

I've always had the challenge of balancing motherhood with my career. My sons were active in sports and other school activities, and priorities sometimes collided. But nevertheless, short of some kind of emergency—for example, the school nurse calling about a sick child—I always tried to organize my personal life so that when I *was* with my customers, they felt that I lived and breathed for them.

**6. Don't get off the subject.** Conversational detours can be toxic to the sales process. Granted, it's good to explore common ground with your customer, and building a rapport is an important part of selling. But if, say, you're in real estate and you find yourself talking more about your kid in college than your customer's housing needs, you've gotten off course.

Getting off the sales topic is counterproductive for two reasons. It eats up time, which you *and* your customer have a limited amount of, and it sends a message to your customer that their needs aren't a top priority to you.

A while back, a television-advertising executive made a mistake with one of our dealership's sales managers. He invited the sales manager to lunch for the purpose of discussing the benefits of our dealership making a longer-term advertising buy. I was interested to hear the results of the meeting—and to learn how much more cost-effective it would be for us to purchase advertisements once every quarter as opposed to monthly. You can imagine my disappointment when the sales manager told me that the subject "barely came up." It seems the executive consumed the time during lunch (along with the travel time to and from the restaurant, since they met at one of our dealerships) with talk about cars. Not car sales, but cars in general—everything from classic cars to race cars. But never a word about what his product—TV exposure—might do to improve the sale of our new cars. I suspect that he was trying to segue his way into his agenda, but got sidetracked. It was not a successful sales call.

**7. Never embarrass your customer.** Whether you notice spinach in your customer's teeth or a shirt button that's unfastened, be sensitive about calling attention to anything that might cause your customer discomfort.

I was at a meeting with a cosmetic company's team of executives to discuss the possibility of my conducting a series of sales workshops for them. One of the gentlemen in the room had a suit-jacket collar flipped up during the entire course of the meeting. Rather than embarrass him in front of his peers, I tried to ignore it. At the end of the meeting, as everyone was standing up to say their good-byes, one of his partners walked up to him and folded his collar down, telling him, "There, that's better. I've wanted to do that the whole meeting." The rest of us tried to disappear as he blushed with embarrassment. Had I attempted it, rather than his partner, it would have spelled disaster.

If you find it necessary to call attention to someone's faux pas, do it in an aside, one-on-one. It's also better to mention it to them at the beginning of a meeting (with your motive being to prevent them from appearing foolish) rather than at the end (when it's too late for them to do anything about it).

**8. Don't argue with anyone in your customer's presence.** Arguing with a customer is always a mistake. But arguing with *anyone* in your customer's presence can be lethal to the sales process.

My friends and I were at a Japanese restaurant where the chef flamboyantly prepared our food before us. The manager came up to him and discreetly attempted to reprimand him for having gone to the wrong station. The chef pulled a piece of paper from his pocket and offered it as evidence that the mistake was not his. Their whispers, back and forth, grew louder. (I feared at one point that the shrimp and chicken on the grill in front of us were going to burn.) Who was right in the context of the argument? I never knew. But I believe they were both wrong to stage their argument within earshot of the very people they were attempting to please. It cost them both—in tips and in future business.

**9. Don't use turnoff words or phrases.** Every generation seems to adopt a language of their own. The problem is that when it spills over into adulthood and enters the business world, generational jargon can be offputting. The word "like" comes to mind. "*Like*, I mean, do you want a four-cylinder or a six-cylinder?" "*Like*, how set are you on owning a red one?" Use of proper language is a plus in sales.

Other phrases, such as "you know," project a sense of insecurity. "You know" is usually delivered at the end of a sentence, slightly turned up like a question. "This car offers great value, *you know?*" "This is a good time to buy a house, *you know?*" I once heard a Hollywood celebrity being interviewed, and almost every answer she gave ended with a "you know?" What listeners hear is the speaker's need to be confirmed on their answer—as if they are not sure of it themselves.

And if you're truly being honest, you'll never have to use such phrases as "To tell the truth . . ." or "Let me be honest with you . . ." If you use phrases such as this, the natural tendency for a customer is to wonder if everything you've stated previously was a lie.

**10. Don't blab or bash.** What you say *can* be held against you. Whether it's talking in an inappropriate setting or bashing your competition—or anyone else, for that matter—talking out of turn can squash a relationship and a sale. (This is yet another example of the fact that you are always on stage.)

When it comes to talking negatively about someone, it doesn't matter what the setting is, your words always have the potential to come back and haunt you. Even when I'm seduced by customers who tell me what a bad experience they had at a competitor's, I simply offer a dose of empathy and move on. In the end, customers respect you more when you refrain from talking negatively. Stay positive. Always.

**11. Don't accept credit for something you didn't do.** Taking credit for something accomplished by someone else is stealing. It can come back to bite you.

As a sales manager, I was asked at a meeting, along with the rest of the management team, to come up with ways of cutting costs for the dealership. On a lunch break, I told a colleague about one of my ideas. When the meeting reconvened after lunch, the owner of the dealership opened with an announcement about the first change we would be adopting. I couldn't believe the coincidence; it was my idea—*exactly*. As he unveiled it, the owner praised my lunch partner for it. I thought to myself, "What a rat!"

My plan called for a consolidation of the new- and used-car departments. Instead of two separate sales managers and sales staffs, there would be only one. But in the end, the integration didn't work. Soon after the plan was implemented, sales declined, along with employee morale. The manager who stole my idea ended up having to live with a black eye.

**12. Don't oversell.** Once a customer has said "Write it up" or "I'll take it," proceed with the delivery process. The sale has been made. If you keep talking about the product, you come off sounding as if you can't believe the customer has actually bought the product or service in question. Their natural reaction is to start doubting their decision to buy. Even saying something as seemingly harmless as "You won't be sorry, I promise" can be harmful. Can you imagine standing at the wedding altar and— after exchanging vows with your spouse—hearing those words said to you? Of course not. Your reaction would probably be "What have I gotten myself into?" The premise is the same. It's not wise to introduce an element of even potential doubt or regret into what should be a happy occasion.

# Chapter 18

# 12 SURE WAYS TO IMPROVE YOUR SALES

**1. Make eye contact.** This advice may seem obvious, but it's amazing how many sales people overlook it (no pun intended). Visual contact—both when you are speaking *and* when you are concentrating on what the other person has to say—connects you with the person you're communicating with. When you're doing the talking, looking into someone's eyes sends a message of sincerity and honesty. When you're listening, making good visual contact sends a message of interest and caring.

By contrast, looking down, all around the room, or even only generally at the other person's face when you're talking makes you appear as if you have something to hide; looking away when someone else is talking gives the appearance that you're bored.

There is another benefit to making eye contact. It projects an aura of confidence, as I discovered when I was coaching a young salesman years ago. I had just finished telling him that not making eye contact gave the impression he had something he was trying to conceal.

"Ms. Brem, it's not that I have anything to hide," he told me. "I'm just afraid that the customer's going to ask me something I don't know." In a sense, he *was* trying to hide something—his fear of being less than knowledgeable. After pointing out to him that no one—not even the most seasoned sales veteran—has all the answers, I gave him some exercises to rehearse, consisting of looking me in the eye and saying the words, "I don't know the answer, but I will try to find out for you." Once he got comfortable admitting that he didn't know everything (and none of us do), his eye contact with his customers improved dramatically, and so did his sales.

I had a similar experience coaching a female salesperson. She was not making eye contact with her customers when they were talking. Even though she *said* she was listening, she'd be doing other things at the same time—filling out paperwork, entering data into her computer, doing anything but connecting visually with her customer. She told me that her "multitasking" helped her not to interrupt her customers—a weakness she had been working on overcoming. After we talked, she recognized that she had traded in one bad habit for another; as a result, she began to work on how to be still, and not just wait for her turn to talk, but instead really listen. Folding her hands in front of her, nodding her head occasionally, and looking into her customer's eyes when they were talking helped her to listen *actively*. Later, she told me this change in the way she listened made a huge difference for her not only at work but at home with her family as well.

Whichever side of the conversation you're on, by making

good eye contact, the other person can literally see that you're engaged. The opposite is also true—if you're not making eye contact, your customer will assume you're not engaged or connected. And where there is no connection, there is no sale.

**2. Smile.** Smiling is a great communication tool. It projects three things: confidence, enthusiasm, and acceptance of the other person.

It's rare you see an insecure person smiling; that's precisely why it conveys confidence. But to take it one step further, I have found that even during those times when I am feeling a bit unsure of myself, by smiling, I am actually able to bolster my self-confidence.

The same is true if I'm feeling a little blue or under the weather. When I smile, I'm able to generate a feeling of well-being, which often makes me happier.

I recognize that at times it's hard to smile—if, for example, your heart has just been broken. At such times, be gentle with yourself; nurture yourself as you would a dear friend.

That being said, finding happiness *is* an inside job. It begins with a decision only you can make: Today, I'm going to be happy.

Happiness and enthusiasm go hand in hand. Moreover, they're contagious. If you're enthusiastic about being wherever you are and doing whatever you're doing, people around you tend to join in. And it's so much easier to do anything—including buying and selling—in an environment of enthusiasm.

Smiling at (and with) someone conveys a feeling of excitement and acceptance. It is similar to a dog wagging its tail. (You dog owners—think of the good feeling you get walking through the door and being greeted by your dog's enthusiastic tail-wagging.)

When you smile at customers, they feel they're being

accepted. They feel safe to let their hair down, so to speak. It becomes easier for them to talk about their wants and needs. For you, this leads to being better able to help them.

**3. Use the telephone effectively**. There is no substitute for selling face-to-face. The most advanced technology can never reproduce the good feelings generated by a handshake, eye contact, and a smile. But the next best thing to being there in person is a phone call.

Traditional mail, text messages, and e-mails are helpful communication tools, but I feel a salesperson's utilization of them should be driven more by our *customers'* convenience than our own. In one of my dealerships, I overheard a salesman being asked by his manager if he had contacted his customer to inform him that a car he had shown an interest in now had a rebate offering. He responded, "Yes, I sent him an e-mail." When I asked the salesman why he hadn't called the customer, he told me, "I've been so busy. Sending an e-mail was more convenient."

Here was a case of a salesman passing up an opportunity to be a personal bearer of good tidings, as well as a chance to answer any questions that the customer might have about the rebate offering. After we talked about it, he followed up by calling the customer. Sure enough, the e-mail had raised more questions for the customer than it had answered. (How long was the rebate in effect? Would it affect the financing special he had been offered? Did the rebate apply if he got the "luxury package"?) Because the salesman made the phone call, he was able to address all of the customer's concerns—and make a sale.

Here are some tips I've learned over the years that can enhance communication between you and your client over the phone:

- *Stand*. Standing, as opposed to sitting, energizes your voice. You'll sound more alert and attentive.
- *Smile*. Your client may not be able to see your smile, but they'll *feel* it. You'll sound upbeat and positive.
- *Dress*. For those of you who work from home, making a sales call *after* you've showered and dressed puts you in a better frame of mind than making one in your bathrobe. And when you feel better, you'll do better.
- *Minimize distractions*. Background noise (e.g., a television or a radio) is annoying and disruptive. Without distractions, you're better able to concentrate on your client and their needs. I recall a freelance writer for a women's magazine who kept putting me on hold to tend to her crying baby while she was interviewing me. When she'd return to the call, she'd tell me how hard it was juggling her career with motherhood. I felt sorry for her, but I'm certain she didn't get the best interview. She would have been better off to schedule an appointment for the phone call during the baby's naptime, or when she could have arranged for child care.

**4. Make your cell phone a friend, not a foe.** Offering your business associates and customers your cell phone number gives them meaningful access to you. Indeed, use of a cell phone can be a great sales tool. But if it is used incorrectly, even your best intentions can't overcome the negative fallout.

While I was shopping recently, on three separate occasions the saleswoman I was dealing with said "Excuse me" as she walked away to answer her vibrating cell phone. I left without buying anything.

Cell phones are all but outlawed in movie theaters, restaurants, and other public places. The same premise that holds true there should hold true in the sales process as well. If you opt to respond to a cell phone call in the presence of your customer, you're in essence saying, "Right now, something else is more important to me than meeting your wants and needs." That is something you never want to say.

**5. Get back to your customers promptly.** In the real world, this one's hard. How do you call a customer back promptly when you're busy giving your undivided attention to the customer you're with? I learned early on that I needed systems, as well as the support of other employees.

The switchboard operator who handled the calls at the dealership where I first worked was someone I counted on and always showed great respect toward. I made sure that she always knew where I was and what to do with my calls when I was not at my desk.

When you're not in a position to take a call, e-mail, text message, or other communication from a customer directly, it's helpful if you have someone who can intercept the communication. And you want to make sure this person is in the know as much as possible. At the very least, the person trying to reach you should be told when you'll be available—for example, back from vacation, back in the office, or on shift.

Today, I am fortunate to have a support team to help me implement the systems I have created for handling everything from my mail to my phone messages. My two executive assistants, Gracie and Hope, know precisely what to do when someone is trying to reach me and I am not readily available. They offer the customer a way to obtain immediate help—via a team of department managers, not to mention my two sons, Brannon and Travis, both executives inside the dealerships, empowered to address and solve *any* customer-service matter. When I am the only one who can respond to a caller, whoever takes my call makes sure the person trying to reach me knows when I can get back with them. For example, if I'm on a four-hour afternoon flight, the caller (or sender of an e-mail) is informed that they will not be hearing from me until first thing the next day. This way, customers are not left in the dark.

Before I had such support, I borrowed an approach from an extremely successful saleswoman I know. She has only voice mail at her disposal, but she changes her voice message daily to fit her schedule. She also checks her messages regularly and schedules a time to return calls, something she gives high priority to. She would usually set aside one hour a day to make calls and send e-mails. Typically, she does this from two to three o'clock so that she has time remaining in the day to take action on a call if necessary. By setting up a schedule like this, you'll be able to avoid the feeling of frustration that comes from looking at your watch only to realize that it's too late to get back to someone.

The busiest salesperson or executive can establish a way to communicate with and help their customers even when it can't be done directly. Set aside a regular time to return client calls. It's a good way to make sure that no one is neglected and that no sale falls through the cracks. Work to create your own system—one that works for you. But make sure you have one.

**6. Keep old relationships alive.** We've heard all of our lives not to "burn bridges." Well, I believe it's even more important to keep the bridges in our lives in good working order. Relationships are vital in sales (and in life). Once you've cultivated one, don't let it wither away. There's an old saying that you meet the same people coming down the ladder as you do climbing up, so it's important not to climb over someone's back. But it's also important to put an effort into continuing to reach out to someone who made a positive difference in your life.

Sending a Christmas card to someone from your past is one way to do this. But I have found that this is a gesture that easily gets lost in the crowd of other card senders doing the same thing. I prefer sending birthday cards or "just because" cards to people I have relationships with. If there's something in the news that reminds me of an old acquaintance, I send a clipping with a "this made me think of you" note. Demonstrating your thoughtfulness is not hard, and the by-product of your act will be twofold. It keeps you in the minds (and hearts) of old friends and acquaintances, and it keeps your spirit of gratitude alive. I know that when I am feeling grateful to someone who's helped me along life's path, I find myself in a more positive frame of mind. And that's a great state to be in when you're making your living in sales.

**7. Be generous and sincere with compliments.** Complimenting someone makes them feel good. Yet many of us are reluctant to compliment someone for fear that doing so will come at an expense to us. Maybe we'll look foolish, or the compliment will come off as "fake." We even burden the word "compliment" by prefacing it with the word "pay" to describe the act.

Well, a compliment is not something you "pay" someone; it's something you *give* them. It doesn't cost you anything. Nor should you expect anything back from it. I know improving sales is the subject of this chapter, and complimenting your customers—along with adhering to all of the important fundamentals previously discussed—can help you to do that. But when complimenting is done sincerely, it comes with no expectation of a return.

One way to offer a customer a compliment is by commenting when you catch your customer asking good questions and making intelligent comparisons: "You've asked me a good question" or "You've made a good comparison." Phrase the compliments in such a way that the listener can feel ownership of his or her good act(s)—use the word "you" as opposed to saying "That's a good question." It's their question. They are the one who made the comparison.

I like to praise someone for an action or a deed rather than for a personal attribute (e.g., nice hair, beautiful eyes, a pretty smile) that may have more to do with genetics than deliberate effort.

Be generous. Hearing a compliment can generate a warm appreciation within the person receiving it. And that may make them more receptive to your suggestions during the sales process. But again, be sincere; people can detect a phony compliment in an instant. Don't expect anything in return—just enjoy the other person's appreciation.

**8. Carry a pen or pencil at all times to aid your memory.** I am a big believer in jotting important information down. My pencil has proved over and over again to be sharper than my memory. For me, not even Palm Pilots and laptops can replace a pen or pencil and a piece of paper. For one thing, it's not always convenient to carry or access a PDA, tape recorder, cell phone, or other electronic gadget. And even the smallest handbag or pocket can accommodate a pen or pencil and something to write on. Even at black-tie events, I make sure I have a pencil with me. When inspired by something someone says in a speech or a comment made by a colleague, I make a record of it that I'll be able to refer to later.

I've been told that I am a good user of information. All of us can be, but first we have to recall the information. I surely could not be an author without employing this little trick. (When I'm writing, I stay alert for inspiration in the most unlikely situations—e.g., ball games, golf matches, dinner with friends.) And I know that the notes I've taken of points made during phone calls, meetings, and conferences have helped me to complete many a sale.

**9. Self-motivate.** In sales, we're charged with providing the motivation for someone to want to purchase our product or service. But who motivates the motivator? That, I have learned, is *my* responsibility. But I don't have to do it alone.

I make a conscious effort to surround myself with upbeat people. People's moods (unless you're a robot) affect you. It's important to seek out a positive environment for yourself. Even in my early selling days, I chose to stay away from "the point"— the outdoor corner of the dealership where salesmen congregated while waiting for customers to drive up and talked about all of the wrongs in the world (the unfair pay plan, sluggish business, stupid customers, and so on). When I can help it (and that's most of the time), I choose optimistic, grateful, and cheery people to breathe the same air with. I have learned that my environment—the people around me—is one of my greatest influencers.

In the same way, I seek out books, tapes, and other media that help me to refuel. "You are what you eat," we've all been told. That is true of what our minds ingest, too. Depending on what I put into my Walkman, I can leave a plane after a long, crowded flight feeling either exhausted or energized. The choice is mine.

Sometimes, before you can take in good information, you need to delete the junk. This is where "letting go" comes in. Did someone wrong you yesterday, or yesteryear? Maybe you were laid off unfairly, or a girlfriend left you for someone else. Perhaps growing up you felt your parents liked your sister or brother more than you. Do you find yourself replaying the events of your life in your mind as if doing so will produce a different outcome? It won't. My advice is to forgive and move on—for your *own* sake. The unfair people in my life might have affected my past, but I'm in charge of my present and future.

Additionally, expectations play a role in our happiness. I understand that sales slumps are part of my profession. I have found that when I have prepared for them, when I expect and anticipate them (e.g., by putting money aside), I am much more able to navigate my way through them. My mind is able to focus on the solution, not the problem.

In sales, there are always bumps in the road. Prepare for the inevitable downturns. Then work harder; instead of making three sales calls a day, make four. Instead of working your shift, go into the office early. There is no substitute for hard work. What naturally follows when we combine hard work with a positive attitude is success.

The natural ebb and flow of sales means that you will always be challenged. How you respond to those challenges is greatly influenced by your state of mind and your energy level. That's why you should always pay attention to your physical well-being; its impact on your mental and emotional health is too great to ignore. I don't claim to be a nutritionist or medical expert. But I know that if I don't take care of myself, I can't take care of others. When I am energized, I feel invincible. I am able to get an early start in the morning, go full speed throughout the day, and come home with fuel left over.

Proper nutrition, exercise, and rest, for me, are *not* optional. For those times when I have to eat on the run, I keep a small refrigerator stocked with healthy fruits and snacks. I carve time out for myself to exercise and wind down.

You know what works best for you. The essence of my advice on this subject is to take care of yourself first.

**10. Ask.** Everyone who has enjoyed some success in their profession is asked at one time or another for their "recipe." So here goes Marion's Principle: *Always work beyond expectations, and find someone who notices (even if you have to ask to get their attention).*

The first part of the principle seems to come easy—especially for women, who are trained almost from birth to be people pleasers.

But finding someone to "notice" can be hard. I've divided Marion's Principle into three steps: They are sure ways to improve your sales.

*Step #1 is to ask.* I'd been selling cars for two years, earning every award and recognition my position had to offer. The only records left to be broken at the dealership where I worked were my own. I wanted to share my experiences with others, too, and so I *asked* for a promotion to management. The sales manager told me no. The general manager told me no. The CEO told me no. They seemed to share a consensus that my greatest value to the organization was right where I was, in selling, not management. In the end, I had to ask elsewhere. Another auto dealer took a chance and hired me in spite of not having any management experience. But my ultimate success at finding the promotion I wanted came about because I first asked.

My experience has taught me that we might not get everything we ask for, but we do miss out on many things we don't ask for.

Let me give you another example. An expansion of our dealership's sales force prompted us to advertise for qualified salespersons. After two weeks of conducting interviews, the general manager reported to me that out of twenty seemingly qualified applicants, he had hired only two. He went on to tell me that they were the only two who had asked for the position. (Only 10 percent!) His thinking (one I share) was that if a salesperson didn't ask for the position—because of fear of rejection, timidity, or ambiguity about really wanting the job—how could they be relied upon to ask for the sale?

The professional world is not like it was for us in school, where if we did all of our work we automatically got promoted to the next grade. In business, and especially in sales, only occasionally will doing what's expected (e.g., submitting a résumé, showing up for an interview, meeting the demands listed on our job description) advance us to the next level.

I have learned that there are as many ways to ask for a sale as there are customers. But the common denominator behind success is timing. Ask for the sale *after* you feel you've exceeded the expectations of the prospective client; it is much easier, and your success rate will be much higher. Learn what your customer expects—regarding delivery time, price, setup, assembly, product capability, service after the sale, perks associated with making a purchase (e.g., becoming a member of a frequent-buyer club), guarantee, warranty, return policy, and so on—then set out to exceed it.

Say a customer's indicated he or she would like to be driving a new minivan by the weekend. It's a lot easier to ask for their business after you've told them they can drive it home that day. Say your customer tells you they need a computer that does X. If you're able to show them that the computer you sell not only does X but it also does Y, you're in a good position to ask for the sale.

When, and only when, you feel you've met the standard of not merely satisfying your customer but, rather, delighting them, ask: "Is it safe for me to assume that I've earned your business?" or "Shall I call the manufacturer to place your order?" or "How many would you like?" or "Are you happy enough with the terms for me to proceed?" Whatever words you choose, the important—no, the critical—thing is that you ask for the sale.

Remember, people really do want to say yes. We've all heard the saying "Be careful what you ask for; you might get it." It's true. I remind my sales staff frequently that people who step foot onto our car lots have "new-car fever," and that we have the cure. All the salesperson has to do before they ask for the customer's business is to learn what the customer's needs are and then set out to exceed them.

**11. Get the word out.** (This is Step #2 of Marion's Principle.) Create venues to let people know what you can do for them. Get the word out. When my request (asking) for a promotion from salesperson to sales manager was met with resistance, I applied elsewhere. I put myself (along with my résumé) "out there." I let other prospective employers know that I was available, and that I was capable of making a positive difference in their businesses. I started out by making phone calls to other dealerships in the area. But I didn't stop there. I called friends (at affiliated businesses like banks and advertising agencies) that I had made in the two and a half years I had been selling cars. I asked them to put the word out that I was "in the market." It was almost like pollinating the automotive community with my message. About a month later, I found someone who appreciated my past accomplishments and potential. And it all happened because I got the word out.

When I wanted to advance from management to ownership, I sent a folder of information on myself out to prospective investors—another way in which getting the word out has worked for me.

A service greeter in one of my dealerships expressed an interest in learning more about the business. She first asked the service manager about the possibilities of a transfer to another department—for example, the accounting department—so she could be exposed to other parts of our operation. He expressed an appreciation for her ambition and told her he would keep her request in mind. Knowing that she needed to get the word out to other department managers—and at the same time not offend him—she asked him if it would be possible for her to have some time at the next manager's meeting to introduce herself and let her desires be known. He honored her request; after making her presentation (short but complete, explaining how much she loved the business and stating that she wanted to make a career for herself in it), she was transferred to the accounting department. Since then her career has progressed rapidly, and she has been a great contributor to the dealership.

Ask yourself how you can better let people know about *you*—your product and services. And girls, I write this for you, since we tend to be more reticent then men: Don't be afraid to brag a bit (as long as you don't exaggerate). If you have a means of getting the job done that your competitor does not possess, don't keep it a secret. Get the word out. Remember that standing out from the pack in this sense is a good thing. A "me, too" approach won't get you where you want to go.

Create a brand for yourself. One enterprising Realtor I know claims to be a "first home specialist." Knowing that newlyweds are, or soon will be, in the market for a home, she gets the word out about her specialty (her brand) by telling wedding planners about her area of expertise (complete with access to first-time-homeowner mortgages, no-closing-cost financing, etc.). Because they know and like her, she gets many referrals that way. She recently set up a booth at a bridal fair, where she offered a promotion that included a honeymoon package with the purchase of a home. She·even worked out a deal with a travel agent (for the honeymoon packages), who in turn refers clients to her. He told me that he learned (almost) firsthand from his son's home-buying experience that "she's great with young people." Her business is booming, not only because she created a niche for herself but also because she doesn't shy away from telling people that she's good at what she does—and what she can do for them.

**12. Stay with it.** (This is Step #3 of Marion's Principle.) Follow up, follow up, and follow up some more. Otherwise said—stay with it.

As a sales manager, I conducted a study of the sixteen salespeople who worked for me in order to learn which ones possessed the strongest "closing ratio" (transactions as a percentage of prospects). The purpose of my study was to determine what it was about the high-volume salespersons that made them earn more. Were they playing the numbers game and simply talking to more people, or were they just more talented? I figured if I could pinpoint what it was, I could better help the salespeople who were not enjoying the same level of success, and thereby increase the overall sales volume of the dealership.

For two months, I had them make a record of their daily activities. Included in their sales journal were the customer's name, the type of contact made (phone, in person), the source of the contact (referral from another customer, friend, relative, or a new phone inquiry), the result of the contact (sale, missed sale), and other pertinent information. To this day, my findings remain one of the greatest revelations in my career. The top two salespersons (the ones who had the most sales) talked to the *fewest* sales prospects! They simply talked more often to the *same* sales prospects. In other words, they hung in there longer with the same people. When I examined my findings more closely, I learned that in some cases they had asked the customer *five times* for the sale.

I thought back to my days when I was selling cars and realized that I, too, had done the same thing. In fact, the nicknames that had been given to me by my colleagues were a testament to my stick-to-it-tiveness—"Gummy Bear," "Miss Doesn't Give Up." If one car didn't fit a customer's budget, I'd call them back with figures on another. (Even if they had declined considering another when they learned their dream car was not affordable, I knew that after some time passed, they might reconsider.) If we weren't able to give them as much for their trade-in as they wanted, I'd try to find a buyer for it myself. If we didn't have a car to meet their needs, I tried to find them one at another dealership (and then persuade my management to make a swap with the other dealer for it). I worked *every* deal from *every* angle. I never engaged in any pushiness or "high pressure" tactics. I was simply enterprising *and* persistent. And that was, and still is, a major ingredient in my recipe for success in sales, *and* in life.

# Chapter 19

# WHY WOMEN MAKE THE BEST SALESMEN

Whenever I've been asked how I've "made it" in a male-dominated industry, I've responded, "Largely, because I'm a woman." For as I hope I've shown you, women *do* have advantages over men in the world of sales.

The first and most obvious advantage, as I've pointed out repeatedly, is the makeup of today's market. Female buyers are no longer a "segment"; they *are* the market. They make the vast majority of buying decisions. The dainty little hand that men once thought pushed only a shopping cart or a baby carriage now has a viselike grip on the economy. *And all things being equal (e.g., price, product quality, and availability), customers prefer to buy from people who are most like themselves.*

Second, the "disease to please" (primarily associated with women)—that is so often pointed to as limiting our ability to sell—has a positive side to it. Pleasing others can be a very effective way of getting people to like you. *All things being equal, people prefer to buy from people they like.*

While men claim to be more focused (and I don't believe it for a second)—they tend to miss surrounding details. By contrast, women are more apt to pick up information important to making a personal connection with someone. Such observation and awareness are powerful in sales. *All things being equal, everyone likes to buy from a salesperson who is intuitive and attentive to their needs.*

Good communication is vital for any successful relationship. Women, by and large, understand this and aren't afraid to apply it. When a woman says to her spouse, "We need to talk," her husband thinks they have a problem. She, on the other hand, probably thinks they have a problem if they *don't* talk. Since talking comes more naturally for most women—and they are more comfortable having conversations—it follows that they have a head start in sales. *Everything being equal, people are more apt to buy from someone who explains things thoroughly.*

And because women tend to be more in touch with their emotions than men, they can use their sensitivities to their advantage. Take rejection. By *reasonably* personalizing it, a sales person can work to do better the next time around, because they are willing to learn from it. As a rule, women aren't ashamed to show their vulnerable sides as much as men. In response, customers are more comfortable reciprocating, and honest exchanges follow. *When everything else is equal, customers prefer to buy from someone they can be candid with.*

## 19.1    For Men Only

If you're a man reading this, first of all I applaud you. You obviously are willing to look outside the traditional (and sometimes) tired information out there.

The important thing to remember is that any of us can learn to develop skills to become better at selling. The motivation is the same for both sexes; once you know how to sell, you have the tools to live your life to its fullest potential—getting more out of it. Because as I've said throughout the book, selling is an integral part of life.

Maybe you weren't born with an "empathy gene." Nonetheless you *can* learn to listen with your heart as well as your head. You can learn to use feeling words (ask your customers, "How do you *feel* about this brand?") not only to stir your listener but also to let them know you support them. A proposed solution, after all, is best understood by a customer when a showing of support from you has preceded it.

Intuition isn't a magical sixth sense. It's a keying in of two senses—seeing and hearing, memory and experience—that all of us, men and women, have. It means seeing not only what's in front of us but what's around us. Hearing not only what's said to us but also what's left unsaid. Hints that help us determine a customer's needs and desires are ever present. The power of intuition is the ability it gives us to predict human behavior. It is a muscle that *can* be developed. Being aware of how strong your sense of intuition is might be a good starting place.

Anyone can exercise the courage to expose their vulnerabilities to another party in a way that brings candor and honesty to a negotiation. Courage is a choice. Sometimes a tough one, but a choice nonetheless. It's not something any of us are born with. Embracing your *strengths* (e.g., being a Mr. Fix-it) is the easy part; becoming aware of your weaknesses takes real courage. Ask yourself: "How comfortable am I with saying, 'I don't have the answer'?" How good are you at offering support when there is no solution in sight? (Do you get frustrated and withdraw?) As much as you like to focus on results (the bottom line), how willing are you to slow down and give new detail to how you present yourself and make your case?

I believe the first step to becoming "stronger" in sales is to admit where we are weak. It's not a matter of *forfeiting* your perceived power; rather, it's a matter of *finding* your *real* power.

Men may have written the first rules of business. That's understandable. They were the only ones allowed to do it at the time. But the rules are being rewritten even as you read this. Now that women make up the majority of the buying public, it is only natural that what once worked in sales doesn't necessarily work anymore. Decoding what women want isn't difficult. It can be learned. And female buyers want to teach you men. Your job is to listen to them. To exercise patience. There is no more valuable attribute in sales today.

Each of us has a huge stake in persuading others of our point of view. Sharing our strengths with one another is critical to the journey. Reconciling the masculine *and* feminine sides of ourselves is one starting place. Working in sales predominantly with men has taught me that true balance and harmony come when we learn from each other. The payoff is more than worth it.

## 19.2    For Women Only

You go, girl. We have what it takes simply by virtue of our gender. Our strengths, nurturing style, passion, and intuition, once discounted in the business world, have now taken hold. Use these special attributes as a means to ignite your self-confidence. When you do, nothing, and no one, can get in your way. The only limits to what you can achieve are self-imposed.

By combining what comes *naturally* to you with today's favorable marketplace—and what you have learned from this book—you should be poised to show your boss, your family, and the world that indeed, women *do* make the best salesmen.

# INDEX

**A**

"A, B, C" reply to defer a
discussion, 91

Allen, Woody, 57

appointment system, 61–64, 68
call-backs and, 62–63
commitment of customer
and, 62
L-I-S-T-S, system for priority
setting, 64
for self, 64

**B**

buyers, emotional makeups of
FASHION CONSCIOUS
passion style, 139–40, 143,
144
NOW passion style, 136–39,
144
RIGHT passion style,
140–41, 144

STATUS QUO passion style,
141–43

buying signs (of readiness to
close), 67–68

**C**

car sales
buying cycle for new cars,
101–2
step selling, 127–28
test drives, sales and, 66–67,
106, 127–28, 137
trust issues in, 150
walking the lot, 19–20
women customers and, 3

Chrysler and Daimler/Chrysler,
89–90, 185–86

closing, 132–33

cold calls, 74

customer(s), 9
anticipating needs of, 26–27

basic needs of, 11

being liked by, six tips, 112–21

bonding with, 117–18

boss or prospective boss, treating as, 4, 11–12, 96–97

buying cycle for new cars, 101–2

complimenting, 200–201

couples as, 3

difficult, dealing with, 159–74

dress of salesperson compatible with, 31–33

emotional engagement with, 55–56

emotional styles of, identifying four basic, 136–43

engaging, 104–5, 107

expressing appreciation, 93

follow-ups, 52–55, 208–10

guiding them through the process of acquiring the product, 14–18, 126–27

"hot buttons" of, 135–36, 145

impressing (*see* salesroom or sales environment)

"just looking," how to respond to, 101–7

keeping old relationships alive, 199–200

liking them first, 120

making a solid first impression on, 51–52, 54, 55

"nonbuyer," 156–57

offer more than they expect, 27

personal information about, collecting and recording, 52–54

preventing disappointment, 18–19, 21

prospecting outside the box, 94–97

prospective, identifying, 9–10

prospective, salesperson's behavior outside the sales arena and, 86–90

recording and using preferences of, 24–25

remembering names, 52

repeat business from, 42–43, 125–26

salesperson's welcome and early arrival for, 59–61

small gestures of caring, 42, 44–45, 59–60

women as, 3, 21–24, 26, 34, 95, 170–72

*See also* difficult customers

**D**

debt, wise use of (and selling yourself to get financing), 78–83

deceptive sales tactics, 183–85

difficult customers

"eternal frat boy," 167

"the hothead," 172–74

humor, keeping and using,
    162–64
"the know-it-all," 168–69
"Mr. Stone Face," how to deal
    with, 165–67
"Ms. Indecisive," 169–72
patience with, 174
universal principles in dealing
    with, 160–62
unsolvable problems, 174
why sell to, 159–60, 174
dress for sales profession
comfort, theirs and yours,
    29–31
compatibility with customer,
    31–33
confidence in, 33–35
guidelines for, 36–37
mimicking others, 33
red, wearing, 35
"Three C's Test" for, 36

E
emotional styles, 135–36
identifying your own, 143–44
See also buyers, emotional
    makeups of
ethics, 86, 150, 183–85
events and sales promotions
"couples" cocktail reception,
    22–23
creating a "wow!" association
    with your business or prod-
    uct, 114

demonstrators and testers,
    106–7
giveaways, 52, 113–14
ladies only, How to Buy a Car
    Clinic, 26, 106
prospecting outside the box,
    94–97
eye contact, 193–95

F
focus groups, 26–27
follow-ups, 52–55, 208–10
heart involved in, 54

H
"hot buttons" of customer,
    135–36, 145

I
image
awareness you are always "on
    stage," 85–87, 97
of confidence and compe-
    tence, 62
creating a brand for yourself,
    208
eye contact and, 193–95
first impression on customer,
    51–52, 54, 55
organization of environment
    and preparedness, 45–49,
    68
personal relationships and,
    69–73

smiling and, 195–96
*See also* dress for sales
profession

L

language
avoiding slang, 128–30
don't use turnoff words or
phrases, 190–91
empathy in, 166, 173
phrases to use with
FASHION CONSCIOUS
passion style, 139–40
phrases to use with NOW
passion style customer, 139
phrases to use with RIGHT
passion style, 141
phrases to use with STATUS
QUO passion style, 143
speaking the customer's, 144
"what" rather than "why,"
171–72
listening skills, using, 24,
100–101, 194
L-I-S-T-S, priority setting system, 64
Love Chrysler, Inc., Corpus
Christi, TX, 5
ads, samples, 86–87, 113–14,
150
cleanliness, internal inspectors system of, 41–42
couples sale, giveaway promotion, 113–14

customer preferences, track-
ing, 25
decor and changing of decor,
42–43
franchise financing for, 78–83
gestures of welcome at, 60
"How to Buy a Car" clinic, 26
name chosen for, 113
organization do's and don'ts
in, 45–48
test drives, overnight, 153–54
test drives, sales and, 66–67,
106
trust issues, 150
"We love your kids" play center, 25

M

making a sale
accessibility to customer,
104–5, 107
adjectives, using during sales
pitch, 114–15
"asking" and timing, 205–6
avoiding a "holding pattern,"
47–48
awaiting arrival of prospect,
tips, 60–61
being helpful to the cus-
tomer, 102–7, 185–86
buying signs (of readiness to
close), 67–68
carrying a pen or pencil and,
201–2

cell phone, as sales tool, 197–98

closing, 132–33

couples as customers, 3

customizing communication for type of customer, 145

eye contact, 193–95

getting a commitment, 63–64

hints and intuition, using, 22–27

"hot buttons" of customer, 135–36, 145

identifying a need and filling it, 6, 10–11, 12

"I'm just looking," responding to, 99–104

inappropriate times and places for, handling, 90–93, 97

ineffective tactics for, 124–25

language, avoiding slang, 128–30

laughter and, 120–21

limiting choices, 131–32

listening skills, using, 24, 100–101

mental ownership of a product or idea, 68

need to be likeable to succeed, 109–21

offer must surpass payment, 11

openers, 103–4, 143

organization and preparedness, 45–49

positive feelings in the customer, creating, 113–15

questions to ask, 130–31

responding to customers promptly, 198–99

secret of high closing ratios, 209

sincerity, 55, 121

smiling, 195–96

"softball question," 130

step selling, 127–28

support team for, 198–99

taking charge vs. taking control, 124–26, 133

targeting women, 95

telephone, effective use of, and, 196–97

"Wow! me" approach, 26

See also negotiation; product; sales mistakes, ten ways to avoid

motivational tools, 202–4

## N

name-dropping

cautions about using, 74–76

cold calls and, 74

proper use, 76–78, 83

tips for, 78

negotiation, 147–58

common ground, finding, 158

deferring a subject until a

later time, 66–67
enthusiasm in, 155–56, 195
ethical code for, 150
first offers, accepting, 157
"frozen" response, handling,
    152–53
good timing, 64–68
invite customer's statement
    of position, 151
learn what works for you,
    155, 158
never underestimate a
    "nonbuyer," 156–57
presenting your offer, 151–52
proceed with assumptions,
    153
product as a "puppy" (cus-
    tomer takes temporary pos-
    session of product), 153–54
refreshments to break the ice,
    150–51
as relationship, 148–49,
    157–58
trust as key, 150
use exact numbers, 153
waiting for customer's reply,
    152
when to part as friends (end-
    ing the negotiation), 154

O
opener
effective, 103–4
question, and emotional style

of customer, 143

P
product, 27
conveying process of
    acquiring it, 14–18, 126–27
as "help" (identifying a need
    and filling it), 6, 10–11, 12,
    185–86
inventory, awareness of,
    18–21, 27
limiting choices and options,
    131–32
as a "puppy" (allowing
    customer temporary
    possession of), 153–54
sharing information about
    (and "just looking"
    response), 104–5
translating specs into
    meaningful terms, 17–18

R
real-estate business
difficult, indecisive customer,
    dealing with, 170
NOW passion style customer,
    mistake with, 138–39
"property showing" prepara-
    tion and early arrival, 60
tips, 44, 46–47
rejection, 175–82
balance in reacting to,
    methods for, 177–78, 182

compartmentalizing feelings and, 178–80

dress inappropriate and, 31–32

externalizing and analyzing basis for, 176, 182

facing and honoring feelings about, 180–81

internalizing, 177, 182

keeping a sense of humor, 163

men, response to, 175, 176

motivation and letting go of negative feelings, 203–4

overcoming fears of, 182

women, tendency to self-blame, 175, 179–80

relationships

A, B, C reply for, 91

accentuating similarities, 117–18

be the bearer of glad tidings, 114–15

bonding through shared experiences, 118

choosing and nurturing, for success, 73–74

expressing appreciation, 93

financing using other people's money (OPM), 78–83

gossip, avoiding, 87–88, 90

keeping old relationships alive, 199–200

let your human side show in, 115–17

name-dropping and, 74–78, 83

need to be likable in, 109–21

opportunities for, and art of persuasion, 92–93

personal advancement and, 69–73, 83, 87–88

receiving, being good at, and, 118–20

successful, and ways to identify you with *their* positive emotions, 112–15

time to sell, and time not to sell in, 90–93, 97

restaurants, repeat customers, gestures for, 60

retail sales

allowing customer to touch the merchandise, 105–6

customer's emotional style and, 143–44

pre-gift-wrapped items, 58

S

S-A-L-E, system to avoid clutter, 48

sales mistakes, ten ways to avoid, 183–93

avoid arguments in the customer's presence, 190

avoid rudeness, 186–87

don't accept credit for something you didn't do, 191–92

don't beg or panic, 187

don't blab or bash, 191

don't get too personal, 187–88

don't lie, 183–85

don't oversell, 192

don't shove customers away, 185–86

don't use turnoff words or phrases, 190–91

never embarrass your customer, 189

stay focused on the sale, 188–89

sales profession

benefits, 6, 7

emotions used in, 55

ethics, 86, 150, 183–85

fear of rejection and, 133 (*see also* rejection)

fields encompassed by, 51

getting hired or a promotion in, 5–6, 11–12, 204–8

need to be likable to succeed, 109–21

qualifications needed, 1–3, 4, 5, 7

women's innate characteristics, how to use to advantage in, 22–27, 72–73, 95, 156, 181, 211–15

salesroom or sales environment

adequate supplies and tools of trade accessible, 47, 49

child care area, 25

cleanliness, 40–45

decor and changing of decor, 42–43

employee morale and, 88

furniture arrangement of, 43

internal inspectors, system of, 41

mirror, use of, 43

organization, benefits of, 45–49

negative effects to avoid, 44, 45

positive attitude about change in, 89

rest rooms, 39–40, 42

S-A-L-E system to avoid clutter, 48

as stage, 39–40, 49

thoughtful gestures for customer in, 42, 44–45

sales slump, overcoming, 202–4

Sewell, Carl, 86

smiling, importance of, 195–96

"softball question," 130

step selling, 127–28


T

telephone, effective use of,

196–97
cell phone, as sales tool,
197–98
changing voice messages
daily, 199
enhancing a call, 197
time and timing
apology for lateness, 59
appointment system, 61–64,
68
asking for a sale and, 205–6
deferring a subject until a
later time, 66–67
early arrival and opportunity
for sale, 57–58
good timing, 64–68
"invest your time to save
your customer's time" rule,
58

job interviews, 61
"no more tardiness" rule, 57
promptness, importance of,
57, 68
psychological disadvantage of
tardiness, 58–59
trust
car sales issues, 150
using with "Mr. Stone Face"
customer, 165–66

© BRYAN TUMLINSON

## ABOUT THE AUTHOR

MARION LUNA BREM was *Inc.* magazine's Entrepreneur of the Year, holds an Avon Women of Enterprise Award, was inducted into the International Automotive Hall of Fame, and was named one of the 100 Most Influential Hispanics in the United States by *Hispanic Business* magazine. She is the author of *The 7 Greatest Truths About Highly Successful Women* and lives in Corpus Christi, Texas.